The Complete Recreational Rower & Racer

The Complete Recreational Rower & Racer

FROM INDOOR ROWING MACHINES TO OUTDOOR SHELLS

STEPHEN KIESLING

Photographs by Jinsey Dauk Kiesling

CROWN PUBLISHERS, INC.
NEW YORK

Published by Crown Publishers, Inc., 201 East 50th Street, New York, New York 10022. Member of the Crown Publishing Group.

CROWN is a trademark of Crown Publishers, Inc.

Manufactured in the United States of America

Library of Congress Cataloging-in-Publication Data

Kiesling, Stephen.
     The complete recreational rower & racer / by Stephen Kiesling ; with photographs by Jinsey Dauk Kiesling. — 1st ed.
        p.   cm.
        1. Rowing.   I. Title.   II. Title: Complete recreational rower & racer.
GV791.K54   1990
797.1'23—dc20   89-28090

ISBN 0-517-57749-6

Book Design by Shari deMiskey

10 9 8 7 6 5 4 3 2

First Edition

For Jennie, my sister,
who introduced me to rowing

CONTENTS

AUTHOR'S NOTE

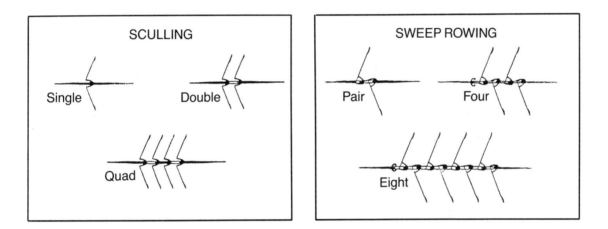

The Complete Recreational Rower & Racer is about a particular form of rowing known as "sculling," primarily in one-person boats called single sculls. I considered using a more technically accurate title *The Complete Recreational Sculler & Racer*, but it proved to be confusing to those who are new to the sport. Scull is defined as:

1. Either of a pair of light oars used, one on each side of a boat, by a single rower

2. A light, narrow racing boat for one, two or four rowers

3. To propel with a scull or sculls—sculler

While it would be technically correct to write: A sculler employs two sculls to scull a scull; for this book I would write: A rower employs two oars to row a single shell.

High school and college programs concentrate almost exclusively on another form of rowing called "sweep" rowing in which each rower pulls with both hands on one oar. After graduation the logistical problems of keeping a crew together forces most sweep rowers to quit. It is my hope that this book will encourage new rowers to take up the sport and former rowers to return to the water in single shells.

INTRODUCTION

Devotees of games often ask why anyone should
take to rowing. . . . Rowing is not a game, it is
much more akin to riding, skating, dancing, or any
other form of locomotion developed into an art.
GILBERT C. BOURNE, *A Textbook on Oarsmanship*

Water attracted me. (L'Eau m'attirait.)
ANDRÉ LANCELOT, French champion

The idea for this book came to me on a beautiful spring morning on the coast of Connecticut. I had been jogging lethargically, knees aching, beside a large pond when I saw a station wagon parked at the edge of the beach. A woman in her late twenties was busily untying the straps that held a bright red Alden Ocean Shell to the roof rack. Alden shells, designed by Arthur Martin in the early 1970s, were the first sliding-seat singles geared for fitness and recreation. I had heard that virtually anyone could hop into an Alden and figure out how to row it within a few minutes—which was exactly why I instinctively disliked them. I had spent about three hours each day for several years learning to row competitively as a member of the Yale crew. The wide-bottomed recreational boats some

how threatened the sport I loved. But I had not been able to row for months, and this Alden was shining like a beacon in the morning sun. I approached the woman, reminding myself of Frank Shields' maxim: "I've never met a rower I completely didn't like." Shields is a former University of Pennsylvania oarsman who has made a career as a corporate headhunter by trading former collegiate rowers around Wall Street. I wondered if his maxim applied to the new breed of recreational scullers as well.

"You look like you need this more than I do," she said shortly. "Why don't you take a turn around the pond." I could have kissed her, but we were at opposite ends of her boat, and by this time I was far too anxious to get out on the water.

My own boat, stored in a boathouse half an hour from home, was a two-man

1

You may think that if you invest a lot of money in a high-tech racing shell that it will be yours alone. But no. Given half the chance, even children can enjoy your shell at least as much as you do.

racing shell called a "pair" built by Empacher in West Germany for the 1984 Olympic trials. The slender 32' hull was built to support our 208-pound averaged weight and still not exceed the minimum weight for international competition. The two oars, oarlocks, and "riggers"—everything including Matthew's size 16 shoes—were made to our specifications. Ted Nash, a former Olympian and Gold Medal–winning coach of the Pennsylvania Athletic Club, helped us fine-tune the rigging to make the boat and oars feel like an extension of our own bodies. Thanks to years of practice, if we had flat water, a straight course, and a light headwind to steady us, we could make the thing fly.

The Alden was built to a different set of standards, and I had always suspected, a different sort of rower. The one-person shell weighed as much as my pair and was wider, yet only half as long. "Stability" and "car-top ability" were words I remembered reading somewhere. There was virtually nothing to adjust and we could set the sturdy Fiberglas hull on the ground while we attached the rigger assembly. She said she had begun to row on a rowing machine the year before, but her boat was almost new: It had taken her only a couple of hours to get comfortable enough to take a full stroke. Now, after about two weeks of rowing, the basic technique was becoming second nature. She loved being on the water and rowing was the best exercise she'd ever had. Together we waded the boat into the pond. I slipped the two sculls into the lock and climbed in.

On my first stroke, a grand sweep of the oars, I rammed a submerged rock—a

I have derived the utmost joy from rowing. Not in any masochistic sense, but in so many positive ways. . . . The assuaging of a burning thirst; the satisfying of a giant appetite; the comfortable tiredness that presages a good night's sleep; the camaraderie of friends all set on the same objective; these things I loved. Then there was that wonderful feeling of fitness, the unleashing of a strength that seemed boundless, and then those wonderful days when the crew's improved technique brought a glorious response in the run and pace of the boat.—GULLY NICKALLS, British champion loud, scraping crunch that would have totaled my Empacher. I mumbled apologetically to the woman and peered over the side: No damage! On my next stroke I was out on the lake. The Alden was wide and stable—it would have taken a lot of effort to capsize it—but it was no rowboat. The "catch" of the blades at each stroke was solid. The stroke was smooth. The shell didn't have the absolute speed of a racing shell, but it ran well between strokes and it felt fast. Within minutes I was caught up in the rhythm of muscles, wooden oars, and water. Legs. . . . back. . . . arms . . . glide! The splash of each catch, the swirls of water rushing by the hull, tracing my path. Glorious! I could see my shadow on the water, so I raced against it, pretending that I was keeping up with John Biglow, my college roommate who placed fourth in the 1984 Olympics in Los Angeles.

After a few minutes I remembered that I was in a borrowed boat, and so I paddled back to the beach and returned it to the owner. The young woman said she had never had a rowing coach and was full of questions. But what amazed me was how easily she moved in the boat. I realized that the Alden had in fact opened up the joys of rowing to virtually everyone. There are now more than fifty different models of recreational shells between the Alden and the flat-water racing shell. And so far, even as the number of recreational rowers doubles and redoubles, Frank Shields' maxim holds true. I have never met a rower I completely didn't like. Not even close.

The beauty of rowing is that virtually anyone of any age can learn. Often the hardest part of rowing is simply convincing a person to get in a shell for the first time. Racing singles look and *are* fragile

and unstable. Entry-level recreational singles are not. Even without the two oars or "sculls" in the oarlocks, an entry-level single will stay upright. Once the oars are in place, the boat will ride comfortably through large wakes and even surf. You can smash into the dock or crash over floating logs without damaging the hull. If you do capsize a single, you realize that it is no big deal. The shell won't sink and you can often climb back in while still on the water. If you can't hoist yourself back into the boat, there is plenty of flotation to keep you safely above water. In fact, most oars have enough buoyancy to support a 195-pound rower.

In the beginning, as you paddle along getting comfortable in the boat, rowing can be no more strenuous than walking. As your technique and conditioning improve, you can pull harder and get a more vigorous cardiovascular workout that strengthens all your major muscle groups: your legs, back, and arms. Rowing is also a remarkably safe way to get fit: You probably won't be able to pull very hard on the oars until you have developed your technique. By that time, your muscles should be ready for the challenge. Unlike other sports, you almost have to begin each row with a long, healthy warmup. Each row requires a new acquaintance with the water. The glorious blending of muscles, oars, and water is only possible if you ease into it. The same is not true, however, of rowing machines and ergometers: You can hop on a rowing machine and flail away without a warmup and without bothering to learn proper technique—which is why so many people who begin their rowing careers on machines end up with sore backs.

Not that many years ago it was believed that rowers risked an enlarged heart and a shortened lifespan. Now we know better. Starting to row at any age will help add years to your life and life to your years.

Even then . . .

Good oarsmanship is not confined to the male sex. —EDWIN DAMPIER
BRICKWOOD, *Boat Racing*, 1876

Rowing at any level requires good concentration. You have to be aware of your muscles, your oars, the water—and you have to look over your shoulders every few moments to see where you're going. The more time you spend rowing, the more instinctual it will become. Good rowing, however, is never completely

The Alden Ocean Shell is classed as a beginning recreational boat—but don't tell that to those who race them.

automatic—which means it is always a good escape from whatever troubles you on shore.

Fine-tuning your rowing stroke will take as much time as you are willing to give it—which is both the beauty and the curse of the sport. Achieving the perfect rowing stroke seems a lot easier than it is. If you have an obsessive, perfectionist streak to your personality, rowing can bring it out.

That day in Connecticut I realized that there is an enormous body of knowledge and lore that would be useful to anyone who dreams of learning to row—especially recreational rowers who teach themselves. Much of this information has already been written down, but it is scattered in manuals and monographs designed for coaches, trainers, and serious competitors. My hope was to gather all the information in one place, listen to the coaches and physiologists, and relay that knowledge with one voice.

My own rowing began as a freshman at Yale. My first strokes were taken in an eight-man concrete boat set in one of Yale's indoor rowing "tanks," motor-driven "rivers" built into the basement of the Payne Whitney gym. After a couple of weeks we were sent out to the Lagoon, a foul swamp on the edge of New Haven, to row in old, wide-bottomed eight-man tubs. In a couple of more months we progressed to the Housatonic River to row in lightweight racing shells. We always raced in eights, but as our technique improved we trained in smaller, less stable boats: four-man shells or "fours," and then two-man boats or "pairs." On rare occasions we went out in singles or doubles.

Not that many years ago virtually all rowers started out in prep school or college in sweep boats (eights, fours, or pairs). This shows the 1979 Yale varsity beating Oxford in the semifinals of the Henley Royal Regatta on the Thames. Seven out of nine members of that crew would row on U.S. National or Olympic teams.

The Yale coaches determined our training and the boatmen prepared our shells. We were not encouraged to learn much about the boats or training for fear that such knowledge might get in the way of pulling hard on the oars. I graduated from college and became a member of the 1980 Olympic Team without ever learning how to set the rigging on a boat.

All sorts of physiological data was collected about me that I didn't really know what to do with. It was in 1981, when I became an editor at *American Health* magazine, that I began to study the science of conditioning. Later, when I had to buy my own shell for the 1984 Olympic trials, I learned about boats. The last part of my education was where many recreational scullers begin: going to the Craftsbury Sculling School in Vermont to improve my technique in a single and build a long-term fitness program.

I should admit that I believe everyone who rows is a competitor. There is great satisfaction in rowing well, but there is greater satisfaction in rowing fast. Win or lose, there is no greater satisfaction than to take part in a race. I hope I can convince you of that: The more racers who compete in a regatta, the more fun it is for everyone.

WHY AUTHORS OF ROWING BOOKS CAN'T BE TOO CAREFUL

Writers tend to be a little fantastical and rowers a little fanatical. The results can be scary, as shown by this historic Cambridge-Oxford exchange.

A very good illustration of the rowing action that develops enough momentum is that of firing a candle out of a gun at a spade. The candle will go clean through the spade and not be in the least hurt, whereas if the candle were pressed against the spade, it would crumple up, just as an oarsman would do if he really dropped the blade in and then pulled. —Cambridge coach Steve Fairbairn, *Fairbairn on Rowing*

To check this statement, I turned down a candle to a good fit in a 12-bore shotgun, and using a full-charge cartridge with the shots removed, I fired the candle at an old shovel. The candle shattered to fragments, but the shovel was not even dented. —Oxford coach H.R.A. "Jumbo" Edwards, *The Way of a Man with a Blade*

NOTE: If you disagree with something in *The Complete Recreational Rower & Racer,* don't shoot! Write me, care of The Rowing Machine Companion.

THE RIGHT SHELL

One of the phone calls that I receive regularly from rowers who have moved to New York City goes something like this:

"Steve, I'm really desperate! I've heard that you row on the Harlem River. Is there a place I can store my shell? If I can't row in this city, I'm going to go crazy."

"Sure, we row on the Harlem," I reply. "What kind of boat do you have?"

"Oh, it's wonderful! It's a custom-made wooden Stampfli I ordered when I was in Europe. It's the most beautiful boat in the world. I have never had a boat fit me so well."

The shell is right out of a Thomas Eakins painting: Light and dark woods blended with superb craftsmanship. It's both a world-class racing shell that you will see in the finals of the Olympics and a boat that you might dream of growing old with. What could be better than rowing a Stampfli with matching wooden oars on a calm, clear Adirondacks lake—leaving the Old Towne canoes in your oar wash.

I imagine the Stampfli on the Harlem: that sleek, delicate hull slicing through a solvent slick on a collision course with a half-submerged refrigerator. Even if the shell survived the river, it would never make it on shore. There is no boathouse, at least not yet, and many of the shells sit out in the open. Life for the Stampfli in New York would be nasty, brutish, and short. I think of the boats that do well on the Harlem, the relatively heavy plastic shells that can be left out in the elements and can ram refrigerators with impunity. Rowing them may not have quite the same aesthetic rewards as rowing a Stampfli, but we get to do it a lot more often.

No matter what your level of experience or your dreams, perhaps the most important consideration when you invest

◄

With smooth water like this, your choice of boat depends entirely on your skill and aspirations. A fast-tracking novice might spend a week of concentrated rowing in a stable beginner's boat like this old Maas Vancouver (center) and then switch to an intermediate shell like the Pocock Off Shore Racer (right). After a year or so of practice, you might be ready to sample the joy of pure speed in a world-class flat-water racer like this Vespoli.

in a boat is where you will row it and how you will store it. Once you decide what sort of boat local conditions can support, take into account your current rowing skills, your aspirations and, of course, what's in your wallet. Even when you have narrowed your choices down that much, you will probably find in the Buyer's Guide at the end of this section that there will still be quite a few different brands to choose from. There is no substitute for rowing several different types of boats. If it is not possible to do that locally, it is well worth the money to go to a rowing camp.

CHOOSING A BOAT

Water conditions: How much water do you have to row? How rough is it? What other kinds of boats will you encounter? Is the water salt or fresh? Are you likely to be banging against rocks or other obstacles? What about tides?

If there are other rowers on your stretch of water, ask around. If not, you'll have to do some research. Figure out

◄

As you progress from beginner to advanced shells, the hulls get longer and more rounded. The bottom of this old Vancouver (center) is wide and almost flat with not much curve or rocker from bow to stern. The Vespoli is round-bottomed. Notice the rounded keel on the Pocock instead of a fin.

when you will be able to schedule your rowing and check the water conditions—including any other traffic on the water. If you row early enough in the morning, even Long Island Sound can be smooth enough for a beginner to handle an intermediate boat. But a few hours later, when the wind and the powerboats churn things up, even a good intermediate rower might want a more stable beginner's boat.

Storage: Most plastic recreational singles can be stored outside in all weather. Sunlight will eventually damage plastic, so it is best to have a cover, but most boats will still last for many years. The more fragile the boat, the more you need a boathouse or room in your garage. Check how long and how wide your storage space is before you order a shell.

CAUTION: Whether you store your boat inside or out, you want a level rack to support the hull. If the rack is not level, even a heavy plastic boat will warp. You can ruin a racing shell fairly quickly with an uneven rack. I learned that the hard way.

Who will row it? Is this boat just for you or will you have to share it? If you buy a beginner's boat, you don't need to answer the question. One size fits all. It is generally possible to make some rigging adjustments to personalize a beginning boat, but even without adjustments, it will be rowable no matter who is in the "cockpit."

As you move toward more advanced and personalized boats, the size, weight, and skill of the rower become more critical. For a husband and wife to row the same boat, for example, the height of the oarlocks may have to be altered between rows. If you progress toward custom, flat-water racing shells, you will discover that hulls come in different sizes for different-size rowers. A lightweight rower in a heavyweight boat may bob like a cork. A heavyweight in a lightweight boat will ride too low in the water and be unable to clear the oars—and may damage the shell.

Stiffness: Even in a beginning shell you want a rigid hull and rigger assembly. A stiff boat will feel smooth and efficient. A flexible hull will wallow, soaking up your energy like a sponge.

The best value in a flat-water racing boat, says boatbuilder Calvin Coffey, is the stiffest hull built to the minimum weight for the least money. Racing shells don't flex much at all. Your smallest movements—for better or worse—are translated directly into the hull. One reason racing shells are expensive is that they use super-stiff lightweight materials such as carbon fiber and Kevlar, which cost more than regular Fiberglas. Kevlar, for example, is about three times stiffer than standard Fiberglas, and costs about three times as much. The shape of the hull also helps determine the stiffness. In general, the deeper the hull, the stiffer it is.

Weight of the boat: The bottom line for beginners is: If you can't carry your shell by yourself, it is too heavy. If you can manage it, don't worry about it too much. Some boats have "drop-in" rigging units to make carrying easier.

In terms of performance for more advanced boats, the weight of your shell is significant—especially in relation to your body weight. The lighter you are the lighter your boat should be. For example,

if a 220-pound rower races a 165-pound rower both in identical 31-pound boats (the minimum boat weight for international competition), the heavier rower will theoretically have a 4-second advantage in a standard 2,000-meter race. On the other hand, the shell that won the 1984 Olympics weighed 36 pounds, 5 pounds more than the minimum. If you have to choose between a lighter and a stiffer boat, choose the stiffer.

Rigging: There are two types of rigging for recreational shells: fixed rigging and removable drop-in units. In a fixed-rigged boat, the riggers, seat, slide, and footstretchers are separate assemblies that are built in or bolted onto the hull. You would expect to carry and store a fixed-rigged boat as is, ready to row. With a drop-in unit those assemblies are all part of a single 15- to 25-pound unit that fastens to the hull with thumb screws or pins. When you transport or store the shell, you remove the unit.

Shoes or clogs: If several people are to use the same boat, you'll probably want clogs instead of shoes mounted on the footstretchers. If you are buying a shell for yourself, shoes are generally more comfortable—and they help ensure that anyone who borrows your boat is roughly your size.

Additional safety features: Aesthetically, you may prefer a boat that blends in with the water. But for safety in crowded waters—or for offshore rowing—you want the brightest color you can find: a color that will raise the hair of even a drunken sailor. If you expect to row in the late afternoon or evening, you'll want reflective tape along your gunnels.

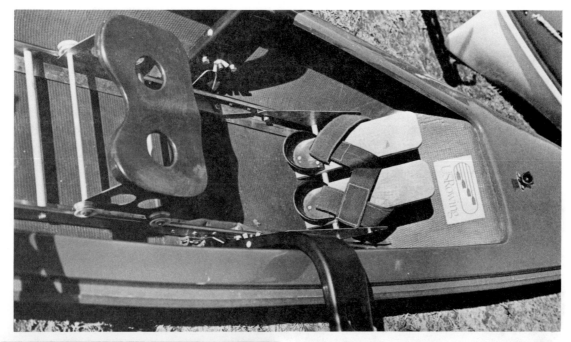

On the Alden, the rigger, seat, and footstretcher are all part of one removable drop-in unit, the Oarsmaster. The unit is adjustable, but you may never notice that you need to. Several different manufacturers make drop-in units so that their shells are easier to carry and store.

The cockpit of this Graham Trimline has clean lines and easy-to-adjust footstretchers.

AND MOST IMPORTANT: If you are just starting out, buy your boat from someone who rows. Recreational shells have become popular enough—and the boat business has become profitable enough—that there are distributors and dealers who know nothing about the equipment they sell. Choosing a reputable manufacturer does not guarantee that your boat will arrive properly adjusted, but you'll have a much better chance.

There are few joys as great as rowing a wing-rigged super-lightweight Van Dusen racing shell with your own shoes mounted on the footstretchers. Of course, you also need the boathouse to hang it in!

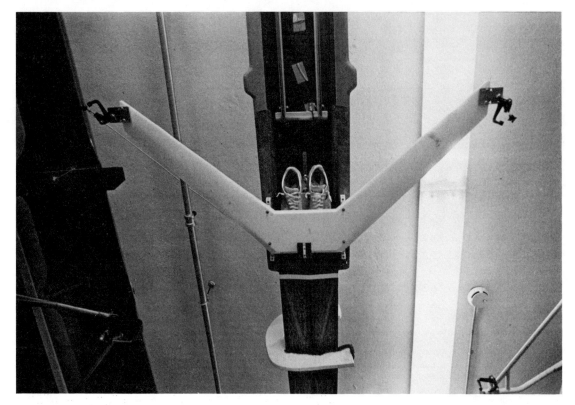

THE PONTOON OPTION

If you dream of a slender racer and your spouse wants more stability, it is possible to buy the narrow boat and a pair of pontoon floats from Hurka Racing Shells that attach to the riggers. Pontoons act like training wheels on a bicycle—about $250.

FLAT-WATER RACERS: TEST FOR STIFFNESS

Here's a test to see if a flat-water racing shell is stiff enough. What you do is support your shell on two sawhorses, place a weight in the middle of the boat, and see how much the hull bends. This test is especially useful if you are looking at used shells and want to evaluate how much they have loosened over time.

1. Find the center of balance of your shell. Typically the center is 14–15 cm toward the bow from the oarlock pins.

2. Support your shell on an even keel with two sawhorses that have a bearing surface of 1½″. The sawhorse should be at an equal distance from the center of balance.

3. Measure the distance from the bottom of the hull at the center of balance to the ground.

4. Place a 20-kg (44-pound) weight on top of the shell at the center of balance.

5. Measure the distance from the center of balance to the ground once again.

If the hull is stiff enough for racing, the second measurement should be within 10 mm of the first for a single and within 8mm for a double.

A SHELL BUYER'S GUIDE

This buyer's guide to recreational shells was created by Greg Sabourin, a former boatbuilder and president of the Northbay Rowing Club in Petaluma, California. The guide divides the shells into three categories—beginning, intermediate, and advanced—according to their length, width, and weight. You will find these classifications a very useful starting point when you set out to buy a shell, but you should also be aware that different "recreational" shells have different pedigrees. Boats like the Coffey Exercise Single, Durham Rec Racer, and Empacher C-Single come from a flat-water tradition. They are the relatively easier-to-row offspring of flat-water racing singles. Boats like the Maas Aero and "24" come from an open-water tradition. A Maas "24" is the open-water equivalent of the best flat-water racing shells.

The beginner recreational shells are all under 20' long and from 18 to 24" wide at the waterline—relatively short with wide, flat bottoms. They are slower than the boats in the other categories, but they are more stable—which makes them easy to learn in. They are also suitable for touring, camping, and fishing. The beginning boats tend to be heavy because the manufacturers want a sturdy boat at a reasonable price. You should be sure that you can carry your shell by yourself. To make transportation and storage easier, several manufacturers use removable drop-in units, complete with riggers, sliding seat, and footstretchers that weigh between 15 and 25 pounds.

The intermediate boats are from 20 to 24' long and from 16 to 19" wide at the waterline. They have a more rounded bottom and more "rocker," the length-wise curve of the bottom of the shell. They are lighter, faster, tippier, and more expensive than the beginner boats. You can learn to row in an intermediate boat, but you can expect to capsize quite often. On the other hand, if you spend a week of concentrated rowing in a beginner boat, you will probably be able to handle an intermediate without much problem.

The advanced recreational boats are 20 to 24' long and only 14 to 16" at the waterline—almost as long, narrow, tippy, and fast as flat-water racing shells. The hulls have a rounder bottom with more rocker. You might expect to spend a year or more in an intermediate before you become comfortable in an advanced boat.

Both the intermediate and advanced boats are probably more versatile than they seem at first glance. They may not have much extra space in the cockpit for gear, but you can still use these boats for touring. Simply put your gear inside waterproof bags and lash them to the deck. Kayakers and canoeists have been doing this for years.

One thing you will notice as you skim through Sabourin's guide is that many recreational shells are very heavy. Fortunately, things are improving. Christian Maas is working on a lightweight beginning boat. Joe Hurka already has one. The new Hurka is made of Fiberglas reinforced with Kevlar. Its hull weighs a mere 22 pounds; with the Piandadosi drop-in unit, it weighs a total of 33 pounds. The secret to its weight is the length—only 14½' (24" at the waterline), which is kept stable by a "fin" that supposedly works like the wing on the America's Cup sailboats. I haven't rowed one, but it sounds very promising and should certainly encourage other builders to make lighter shells.

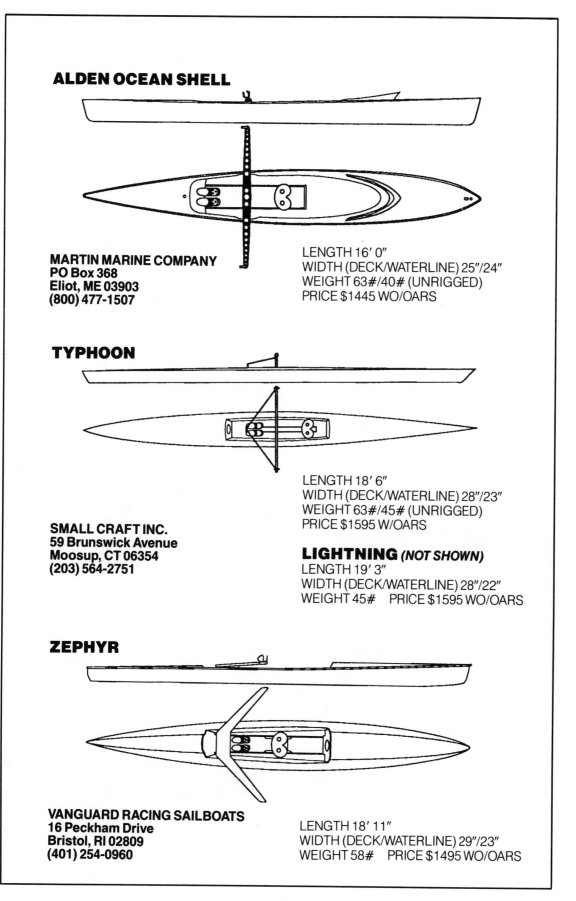

ALDEN OCEAN SHELL

MARTIN MARINE COMPANY
PO Box 368
Eliot, ME 03903
(800) 477-1507

LENGTH 16′ 0″
WIDTH (DECK/WATERLINE) 25″/24″
WEIGHT 63#/40# (UNRIGGED)
PRICE $1445 WO/OARS

TYPHOON

SMALL CRAFT INC.
59 Brunswick Avenue
Moosup, CT 06354
(203) 564-2751

LENGTH 18′ 6″
WIDTH (DECK/WATERLINE) 28″/23″
WEIGHT 63#/45# (UNRIGGED)
PRICE $1595 W/OARS

LIGHTNING *(NOT SHOWN)*
LENGTH 19′ 3″
WIDTH (DECK/WATERLINE) 28″/22″
WEIGHT 45#   PRICE $1595 WO/OARS

ZEPHYR

VANGUARD RACING SAILBOATS
16 Peckham Drive
Bristol, RI 02809
(401) 254-0960

LENGTH 18′ 11″
WIDTH (DECK/WATERLINE) 29″/23″
WEIGHT 58#   PRICE $1495 WO/OARS

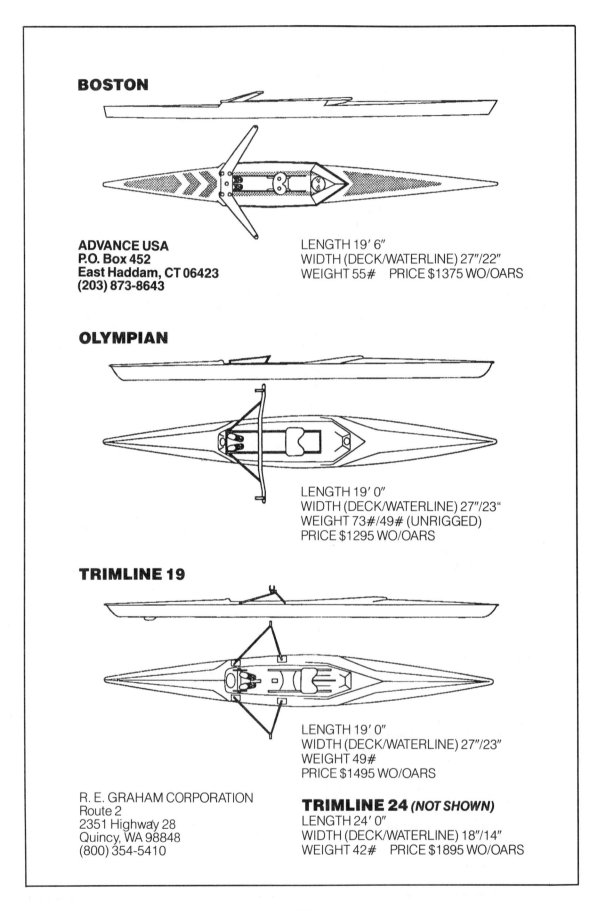

BOSTON

ADVANCE USA
P.O. Box 452
East Haddam, CT 06423
(203) 873-8643

LENGTH 19' 6"
WIDTH (DECK/WATERLINE) 27"/22"
WEIGHT 55#   PRICE $1375 WO/OARS

OLYMPIAN

LENGTH 19' 0"
WIDTH (DECK/WATERLINE) 27"/23"
WEIGHT 73#/49# (UNRIGGED)
PRICE $1295 WO/OARS

TRIMLINE 19

LENGTH 19' 0"
WIDTH (DECK/WATERLINE) 27"/23"
WEIGHT 49#
PRICE $1495 WO/OARS

R. E. GRAHAM CORPORATION
Route 2
2351 Highway 28
Quincy, WA 98848
(800) 354-5410

TRIMLINE 24 *(NOT SHOWN)*
LENGTH 24' 0"
WIDTH (DECK/WATERLINE) 18"/14"
WEIGHT 42#   PRICE $1895 WO/OARS

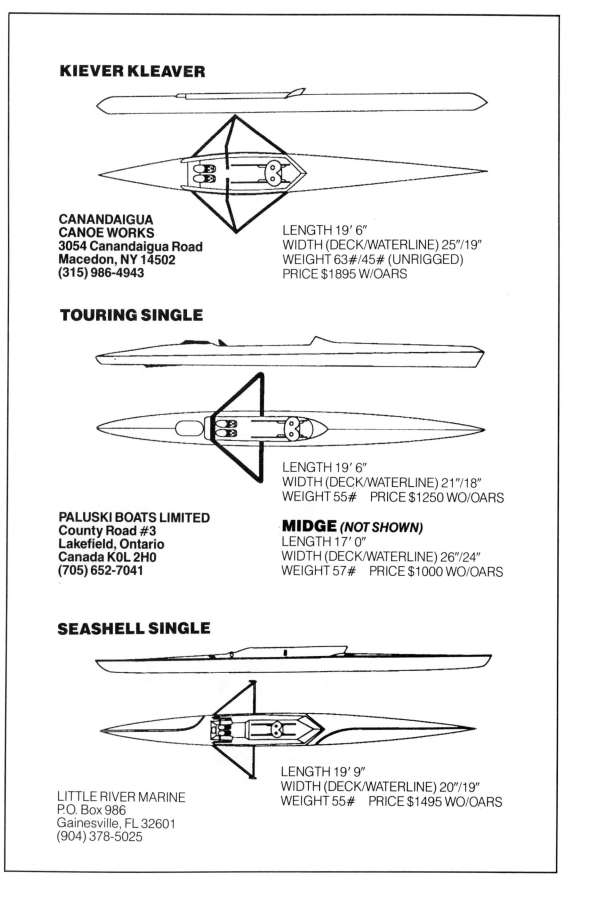

KIEVER KLEAVER

**CANANDAIGUA
CANOE WORKS**
3054 Canandaigua Road
Macedon, NY 14502
(315) 986-4943

LENGTH 19′ 6″
WIDTH (DECK/WATERLINE) 25″/19″
WEIGHT 63#/45# (UNRIGGED)
PRICE $1895 W/OARS

TOURING SINGLE

LENGTH 19′ 6″
WIDTH (DECK/WATERLINE) 21″/18″
WEIGHT 55#   PRICE $1250 WO/OARS

PALUSKI BOATS LIMITED
County Road #3
Lakefield, Ontario
Canada K0L 2H0
(705) 652-7041

MIDGE *(NOT SHOWN)*
LENGTH 17′ 0″
WIDTH (DECK/WATERLINE) 26″/24″
WEIGHT 57#   PRICE $1000 WO/OARS

SEASHELL SINGLE

LENGTH 19′ 9″
WIDTH (DECK/WATERLINE) 20″/19″
WEIGHT 55#   PRICE $1495 WO/OARS

LITTLE RIVER MARINE
P.O. Box 986
Gainesville, FL 32601
(904) 378-5025

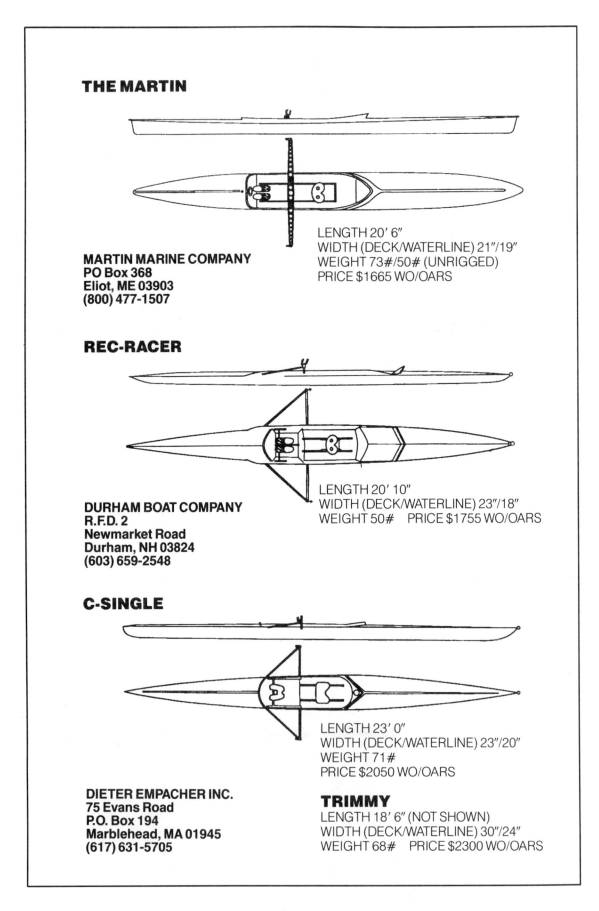

THE MARTIN

MARTIN MARINE COMPANY
PO Box 368
Eliot, ME 03903
(800) 477-1507

LENGTH 20' 6"
WIDTH (DECK/WATERLINE) 21"/19"
WEIGHT 73#/50# (UNRIGGED)
PRICE $1665 WO/OARS

REC-RACER

DURHAM BOAT COMPANY
R.F.D. 2
Newmarket Road
Durham, NH 03824
(603) 659-2548

LENGTH 20' 10"
WIDTH (DECK/WATERLINE) 23"/18"
WEIGHT 50#   PRICE $1755 WO/OARS

C-SINGLE

LENGTH 23' 0"
WIDTH (DECK/WATERLINE) 23"/20"
WEIGHT 71#
PRICE $2050 WO/OARS

DIETER EMPACHER INC.
75 Evans Road
P.O. Box 194
Marblehead, MA 01945
(617) 631-5705

TRIMMY
LENGTH 18' 6" (NOT SHOWN)
WIDTH (DECK/WATERLINE) 30"/24"
WEIGHT 68#   PRICE $2300 WO/OARS

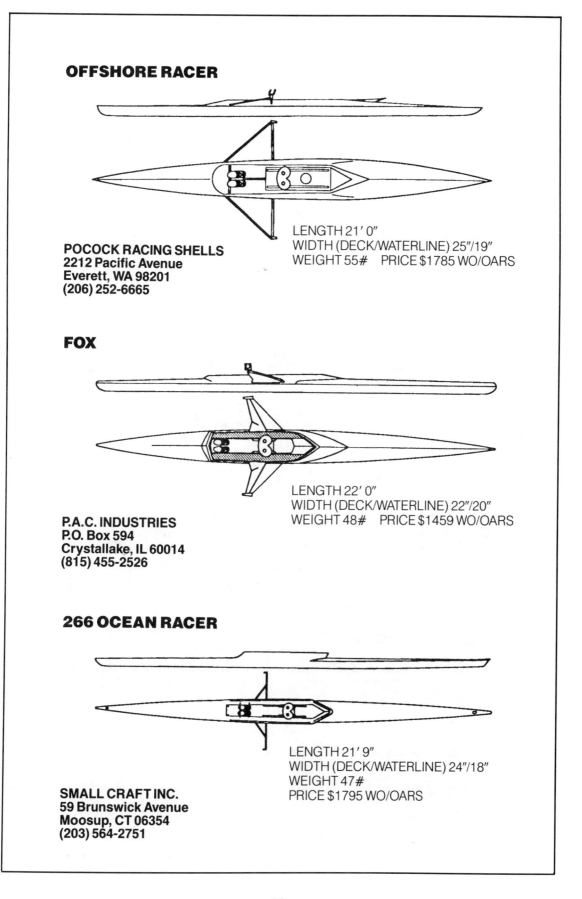

OFFSHORE RACER

POCOCK RACING SHELLS
2212 Pacific Avenue
Everett, WA 98201
(206) 252-6665

LENGTH 21' 0"
WIDTH (DECK/WATERLINE) 25"/19"
WEIGHT 55#   PRICE $1785 WO/OARS

FOX

P.A.C. INDUSTRIES
P.O. Box 594
Crystallake, IL 60014
(815) 455-2526

LENGTH 22' 0"
WIDTH (DECK/WATERLINE) 22"/20"
WEIGHT 48#   PRICE $1459 WO/OARS

266 OCEAN RACER

SMALL CRAFT INC.
59 Brunswick Avenue
Moosup, CT 06354
(203) 564-2751

LENGTH 21' 9"
WIDTH (DECK/WATERLINE) 24"/18"
WEIGHT 47#
PRICE $1795 WO/OARS

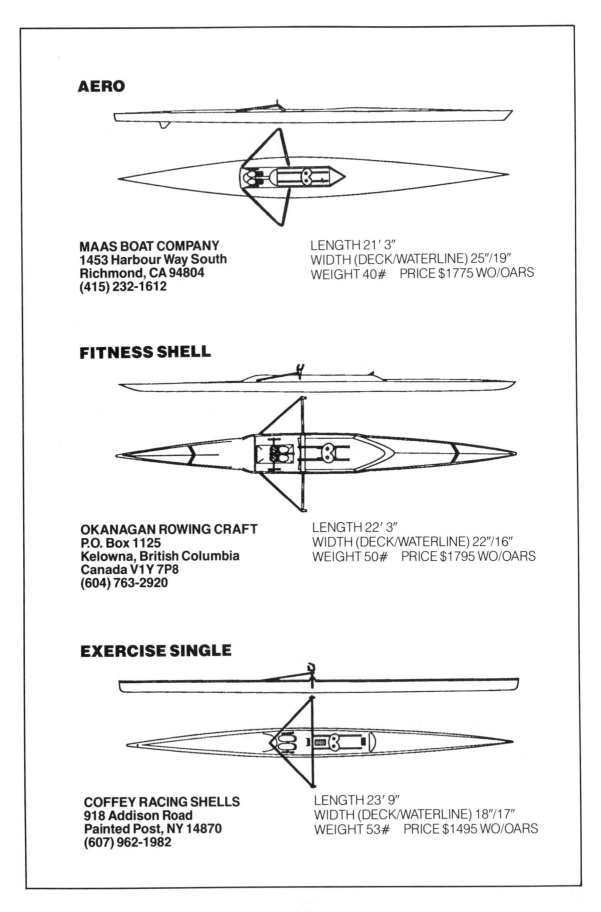

AERO

MAAS BOAT COMPANY
1453 Harbour Way South
Richmond, CA 94804
(415) 232-1612

LENGTH 21′ 3″
WIDTH (DECK/WATERLINE) 25″/19″
WEIGHT 40#   PRICE $1775 WO/OARS

FITNESS SHELL

OKANAGAN ROWING CRAFT
P.O. Box 1125
Kelowna, British Columbia
Canada V1Y 7P8
(604) 763-2920

LENGTH 22′ 3″
WIDTH (DECK/WATERLINE) 22″/16″
WEIGHT 50#   PRICE $1795 WO/OARS

EXERCISE SINGLE

COFFEY RACING SHELLS
918 Addison Road
Painted Post, NY 14870
(607) 962-1982

LENGTH 23′ 9″
WIDTH (DECK/WATERLINE) 18″/17″
WEIGHT 53#   PRICE $1495 WO/OARS

24

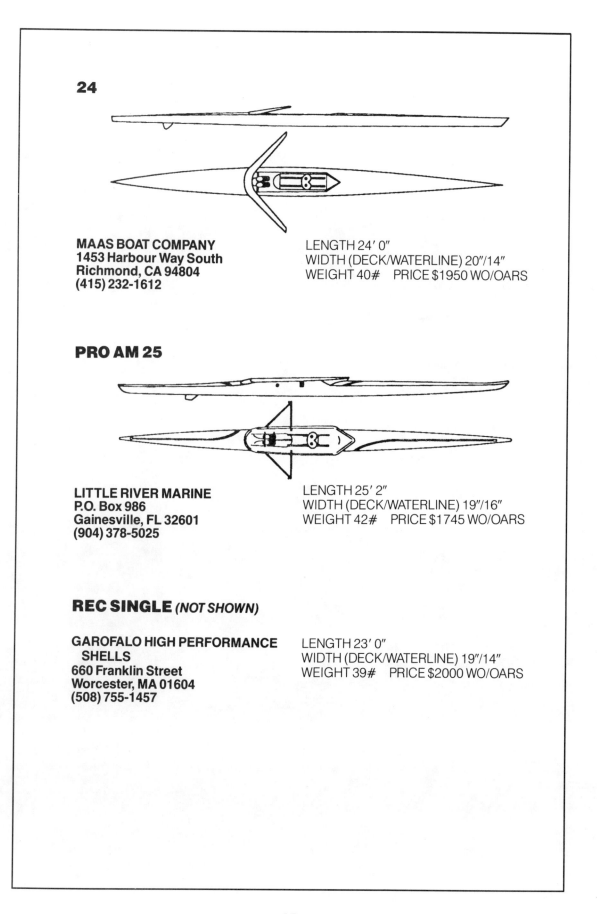

MAAS BOAT COMPANY
1453 Harbour Way South
Richmond, CA 94804
(415) 232-1612

LENGTH 24' 0"
WIDTH (DECK/WATERLINE) 20"/14"
WEIGHT 40#   PRICE $1950 WO/OARS

PRO AM 25

LITTLE RIVER MARINE
P.O. Box 986
Gainesville, FL 32601
(904) 378-5025

LENGTH 25' 2"
WIDTH (DECK/WATERLINE) 19"/16"
WEIGHT 42#   PRICE $1745 WO/OARS

REC SINGLE *(NOT SHOWN)*

**GAROFALO HIGH PERFORMANCE
  SHELLS**
660 Franklin Street
Worcester, MA 01604
(508) 755-1457

LENGTH 23' 0"
WIDTH (DECK/WATERLINE) 19"/14"
WEIGHT 39#   PRICE $2000 WO/OARS

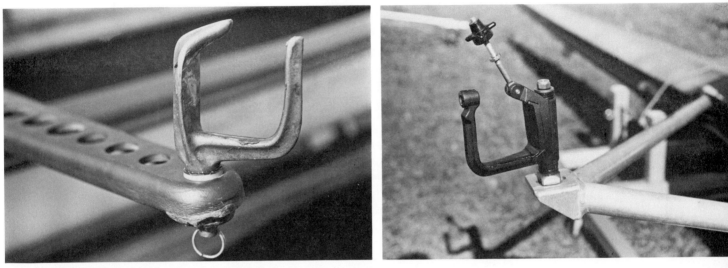

Oarlock sequence: From the simplest oarlocks on the Alden Oarmaster, things become more precise and more complicated.

This woman was moving her boat quite well, but whether that had anything to do with her funny-shaped oar blades is anyone's guess.

CHOOSING THE RIGHT OARS

It seems very simple to choose a good set of oars—and often it is. With many recreational boats, a pair of oars comes as part of the package deal. If not, you just ask your boat dealer or manufacturer for a pair of oars to go with the boat. They may give you a couple of choices to consider, but often they don't. You take what they give you and set about rowing.

But the simplest solution is not always the best. Some of the best oars, like carbon fiber oars from Concept II, are sold by mail from the manufacturer. Retail dealers generally don't stock them, so you'll rarely find them as part of a package. On the other hand, once you go shopping for oars from a manufacturer, you'll be asked a lot of questions: What length oar do you want? How heavy? What pitch? Where do you want the "collar"? How big a blade do you want? How stiff? And then, of course, how much do you have to spend? And finally the manufacturer laughs: "You want these oars when?" It seems like a very simple purchase that suddenly got very confusing. If you are looking for oars in spring or summer, you may have to wait for weeks. You'll wish you had gotten a package deal. If you do push for your own special set of oars, here are the issues that should concern you.

Wood or synthetic: Wooden oars look wonderful, a lot better than even the best of the synthetics. On performance, the jury is still out. I prefer carbon fiber oars, but wooden oars still win plenty of races. Wooden blades tend to be heavier than synthetic materials, but the extra weight can improve the stability of the boat—especially in strong winds or rough water. For durability and ease of maintenance, however, synthetic oars win every contest. Wooden oars should be sanded and varnished regularly. They are fragile and difficult to repair. And they are much more likely to warp when the temperature or humidity changes.

Length: A few centimeters can make a real difference in the feel of the oar. Most recreational scullers are happy with 296-cm oars (9′ 8½″). The same length works well for racers who are less than 5′8″ tall. Taller racers would probably be better off with 298-cm oars. A few very large and strong rowers use 300-cm oars.

Handle diameter: The manufacturer may not ask you about this particular specification, but it makes a lot of difference, especially if you have small hands. You want a handle that fits easily in your fingertips. When you are buying your oars, ask if they have different-size handles.

If the handles you have are too big for your hands, you can remove the rubber grips, sand down the wood, and then replace the grips again. Alternately, you can remove the grips, varnish the wood, and row without the grips. Some rowers like the feel of varnished handles better than rubber.

Weight: At least in theory, lighter oars make for faster boats. On the other hand, the weight of the oars helps stabilize the boat. Unless you are an experienced rower, stay away from super-light oars. Even then, be careful. In rough conditions you may lose a lot more than you gain.

Balance point: You can find this point with your finger. The closer the balance point is to the collar, the lighter the oar will feel in your hand when it's in the oarlock. Check to see that the balance point of both oars is within a couple of millimeters.

Blade size: You may not realize it, but when you pull on an oar, your goal is not to move the oar through the water as it is to move the boat past the oar. The larger the oar blade, the less it slips in the water and the more efficient your stroke becomes. That's one reason oar blades have grown so much in the last thirty years. The standard blade has more than twice the surface area of the old-fashioned oars—and the new oars still seem to be growing. The growth, however, may be getting out of control. I have not seen any good evidence for buying a larger blade than the current standard.

Oar shape: Strangely shaped oar blades seem to come and go. Rowing with them is sort of like shaving your head before a race. Nobody will say you look foolish if you win.

Stiffness: Your oars should flex slightly when you pull on them. If oars were completely rigid, they would be much harder to control and more difficult to get out of the water at the end of the stroke. If you are a novice and can't pull very hard yet, you want flexible oars. The stronger and more experienced you are, the stiffer your oars should be.

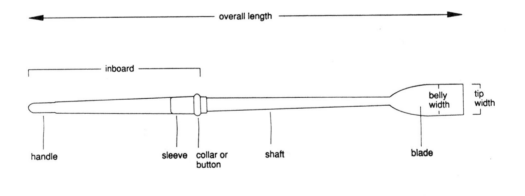

*O*ar blades grow out of all reason, like mushrooms. —Peter Haig-Thomas and M. A. Nicholson, *The English Style of Rowing: New Light on an Old Method*

STEPPING IN ... FALLING OUT; CLIMBING IN ... STEPPING OUT

2

always feel a rush of excitement when I carry a new boat down to the water. It is an awakening, a birth. Rowers can and do make all sorts of jokes about shell-shaped objects, oars, oarlocks, and whatever one wants to make of the water. The symbols are there and must contribute to the profound satisfaction of the sport. But for a novice, that first trip can be harrowing. Your boat will seem ridiculously awkward as you carry it toward the water. Once you set it on the water, no matter how stable your new boat actually is—and most beginning boats are in fact very stable—it will look as if the boat's natural configuration is upside down. Your first lesson, therefore, should be to get in the boat and then to *try* to turn it upside down. Consider this your baptism as a sculler. This may be the only time you ever capsize, but you will be much more comfortable in your boat afterwards. For this first practice, you'll prob-

ably want to wear a swimsuit. You can try this in a large swimming pool.

Safety: The Coast Guard requires that you carry a life preserver for each occupant in a recreational shell, but the only people I know who follow this rule are offshore open-water rowers. A life preserver makes less sense for flat-water rowing—especially when you consider how much flotation is built into standard rowing equipment.

Most any shell will not sink even if it fills with water. If, for some reason, you can't climb back into your boat and row, you should hang onto it until help comes. *Never leave the boat!* If you choose to ignore that rule and swim to shore, take flotation with you. There is probably enough flotation in *each* of your oars to keep you afloat. (Test your own oars: I weight about 210 pounds, and need both of mine to float in fresh water.) No matter how good a swimmer you are, in an

29

emergency, *never* swim from your shell without taking flotation with you.

NOTE: One rower I met was hassled by a Coast Guard patrol for not carrying a life jacket in her boat. She was able to talk her way out of a citation by describing the flotation in the oars.

Quick Checks Before You Carry Your Boat to the Water

Cockpit: Sand smooth any rough edges and cover protruding bolt heads with tape. Make sure that the wing nuts securing the footstretchers to the hull are only finger-tight. Either that or you have a tool with you that will fit them. You may have to adjust your footstretchers when you get into the shell.

Seat: On most seats, there is an opening on one side to make room for your tailbone. Make sure the opening faces toward the bow. Don't feel stupid if you put your seat in backwards. Everyone does. However, it is considered bad form if you don't notice the difference when you sit on it.

Riggers: The bolts should be snug; if your riggers are loose you may damage them.

Oarlocks: The gates or "keepers" that secure your oars in the oarlocks should be kept closed except when you're inserting your oars or taking them out. Open gates flop around and get bent. In a crowded boathouse they poke holes in other people's boats.

Oars: Bring your oars to the water before you bring your boat. Otherwise your boat may float away while you fetch your oars. Bringing your oars down first is especially important if you happen to be at a crowded site where other scullers are waiting to launch.

Fingernails: You may discover eventually that you can row and still sport long fingernails. But when you're learning, cut them short. Also remove any sharp rings.

Carrying Your Shell

The easiest way to carry most shells is with two people. Pick it up from either end near the cockpit—not the ends of the shell. Then turn the boat on edge and cradle it in your arms. If you are alone, the secret to carrying your boat is to find the balance point. Some shells have built-in handles properly spaced on either side of the balance point so you can just grab them and hoist the shell onto your shoulder or onto your head. With other shells you have to feel around to find where they balance.

➤

No matter how sturdy your shell, get in the habit of treating it like a delicate racer. Craftsbury instructor Marlene Royle and the author cradle the boat at each end of the cockpit, not at the ends of the boat.

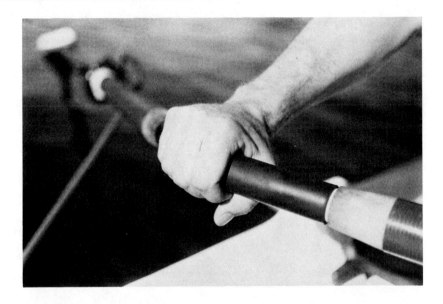

Sitting In

Whether you have a dock to launch from or have to wade into the water, getting into your shell is pretty much the same.

- Put both oars in the oarlocks and secure the gates. Make sure both oar blades are turned flat against the water (or the dock) for maximum stability.

- Bring the tips of the oar handles together so that you can grasp the ends of both handles in one hand. If you pull back gently on the oar handles it will tend to "lock" them together and make the boat stable. Your other hand can rest on the dock or on the rigger.

- Stand beside your shell facing the stern. There should be a nonskid patch or platform designed to support your weight. If you're not sure where it is, find out *before* you step. Otherwise you could put your foot through the bottom of the boat. Put your foot on the platform, shift your weight onto that foot and then lower yourself gently onto the seat.

  When you sit down, you will understand why most seats have two holes or depressions side by side. Wiggle around on the seat until the bones at the bottom of your pelvis drop into the holes on the seat.

  NOTE: If you slouch back in your seat, you won't feel your bones drop into the holes and you won't row properly. If you feel the holes, that means your pelvis is in the proper position, sitting up straight. The better contact you feel with those two holes, the better your balance will be on the water.

- Then place your feet into your footstretchers and "tie in." For proper adjustment, see page 75.

Stepping Out

To exit the shell, just reverse the process: Untie your feet from your footstretchers. Lock the ends of your oar handles with one hand. Bring one foot to the center of the cockpit and stand up on it. Then step out. If you're at a dock, pull in the outside oar as shown (page 35) to help keep the boat from drifting away.

Climbing In: Before you start, insert your oars into the oarlocks and close the gates and turn your oar blades flat against the water. Grasp the ends of the oar handles in one hand and pull gently to lock them together. Put one foot on the platform in the center of the shell. Shift your weight onto that foot and lower yourself onto the seat.

If you must leave your boat at the dock for a few moments, pull the outside oar onto the dock to keep your boat from drifting away.

Flipping Out

After you've spent a few moments practicing getting into and out of your boat at the dock, push yourself away from shore and attempt to flip over. You'll probably find that it is not nearly as easy as it seems. Your oar blades act like pontoons keeping you upright. So long as you hold onto your oar handles, your shell will probably refuse to tip. In a flat-bottomed boat, like an Alden, you can even remain stable without oars. Experiment. Raise and lower your oar handles to see how your balance changes. Shift your weight from side to side. Push the "outside of the envelope" until you go over.

Falling Out: When you realize that you're going to flip, don't fight it—unless the water is very cold. If you struggle to stay upright you may damage your boat or yourself. To get back in, right your shell, if necessary, by reaching over the hull and pulling on the rigger. Grab both oar handles in one hand. Place your other hand between the tracks of the slide. Push yourself up and swing your seat onto the shell.

Climbing In

Right your shell by reaching over the hull and grabbing the far rigger. As you pull the rigger toward you, be careful not to let the oars bash your head. Once the boat is upright, arrange the oars as if you were getting in at a dock: Grasp the ends of both oar handles in one hand, press your body up over the hull, and swing around until you are sitting back in the boat with your legs hanging over the sides. Then simply swing your feet back into the shell, climb back onto the seat, tie your footstretchers, and row away.

Docking: Approach your landing area stern first so you can see what you are doing. Dock upstream (or into the wind) to slow you down as you approach. Back-paddle in and then lean your weight away from the dock and your boat will swing alongside.

Returning to the Dock

As soon as you've changed into dry clothes, you'll learn about the fundamentals of the rowing stroke. In the meantime practice returning to shore. If you are landing at a dock the safest way to approach is backwards. Line up the stern of your shell so that you approach the dock at about a 30° angle "back-paddling," using just your arms. If possible, you should be heading into the wind and into the current. As your stern approaches the dock, lean away from the dock and your boat will gently swing alongside it.

The Classic Way to Carry a Shell

It's easier than it looks. Grasp the gunnel of either side of the boat across the balance point and straighten your legs to bring the boat up to your waist. Raise the boat to your shoulders and then press it over your head. Stabilize the shell by shifting your grasp to the riggers. The first few times you try this, have someone at one end of the boat to help keep you balanced. Don't try this first on a windy day.

The Classic Pickup: Experiment to find the balance point on your hull. Then grasp the hull by the gunnels on either side of the balance point. Use your legs to lift the boat to your waist, then raise the shell to your shoulders and press it over your head. Eventually even beginning-level boats will be light enough to carry this way.

WHY YOU SHOULD TRIM YOUR NAILS

It is often found difficult to keep one hand clear of the other in pulling a pair of sculls. This is so much the case, indeed, that the inexperienced frequently suffer more from the knocking and rubbing of the backs and sides of the hands against each other than from the friction of the handles of the oars in the palms of the hands. —DONALD WALKER, *Manly Exercises; In Which Rowing and Sailing Are Now First Described*

3 THE TECHNICIAN VS. THE HAMMER

You approach your stretcher as you approach your God.—Steve Fairbairn, Cambridge coach

[*Once you've perfected one stroke*] . . . *the same movements have only to be repeated throughout the course.*—Donald Walker, *Manly Exercises: In Which Rowing and Sailing Are Now First Described,* 1838

About four days after my wife, Jinsey, started sculling, she said to me, "If I could row well enough to switch into a skinny racing boat I would beat you." At that time we were spending a week at the Craftsbury Sculling School in northern Vermont. She had plenty of time to watch me in a racing shell and to compare my technique with the camp instructors—as well as see what the world's fastest and most technically elegant scullers looked like on videotape. As Jinsey's rowing eye grew more experienced she looked at my unorthodox style and began to wonder how I moved my boat at all.

There are two basic camps of rowers: "technicians" and "hammers." Already Jinsey had fallen into the first camp: people who for one reason or another look graceful when they row. Her only mistake was to assume that the contortions I go through when I row will neces-

sarily slow me down. You can have a lot of fun hammering your boat along in all kinds of odd-looking ways and still move very quickly—and even win races. On the other hand, it's well worth the effort to try and copy the best technicians.

Jinsey and I were lucky to photograph two U.S. National Team scullers that I had rowed with at Yale: John Biglow, M.D., and Joe Bouscaren, M.D. After college, Biglow won a couple of Bronze Medals at the World Championships and placed fourth at the 1984 Olympics in Los Angeles. Bouscaren has represented the U.S. in the double scull. You can read about the competition between John and Joe in the '84 Olympic trials in David Halberstam's fine book *The Amateurs.* When Jinsey photographed them, they were practicing in their double scull on the evening before the Head of the Charles.

If you watch champion scullers like Biglow or Bouscaren, the most compel-

The Technicians: John Biglow and Joe Bouscaren practicing the night before the Head of the Charles. Note the points of contact: Their weight is centered over the seat, their legs push straight from the footstretchers, and their oar handles ride easily in their fingertips. They remain relaxed even at full pressure, so the shell is not upset by wakes and washes.

ling thing you will notice is how graceful and relaxed they look. The boat seems to travel at a constant speed without lurching fore and aft or wobbling from side to side. The oar blades are in constant movement, following a defined arc like a bicycle chain going round and round. The blades drop into the water and emerge at the end of the stroke with hardly a splash. The only disturbance to the water is a slight wake from the hull and twin whirlpools marking the path of the oars. If you concentrate on their hands, you cannot tell where one stroke ends and the next begins. There's only a slight motion in the fingertips as the oars rotate from squared to feathered position. The legs, back, and shoulders work in a steady progressive sequence to power each stroke and then reverse that sequence to prepare for the next. The head is steady, the face is calm—well,

almost. Every muscle that isn't called into service for the stroke is relaxed.

If you look more closely at the stroke you will begin to break down the rowing cycle into separate actions. You will notice that the progress of the boat is not constant. The shell moves most quickly when it glides between strokes during the "recovery." At the end of the recovery, just before the "catch" of the next stroke, the boat begins to slow down. In fact, the slowest part of the stroke is just after the catch—when the oars have bent under the pull of the rower but have not yet started to move the boat. The boat begins to accelerate gradually as more power is applied.

The sculler's muscles work in concert with the changing speed of the boat. At the catch, when the boat is moving slowest—and feels heaviest—the legs, which are the body's strongest muscles, power the stroke. As the boat begins to accelerate and the load lightens, the back muscles take over from the legs. As the boat accelerates even more, and the load is lightest, the arms finish the stroke. On the recovery, that body sequence reverses itself: The arms swing away from the body, the body swings forward and finally the legs are "cocked" as the rear rolls up the slide for the next stroke.

By now you should feel comfortable getting in and out of the boat and you should not be worried about tipping over. It's time to learn to row.

Release: Your oar handles should just brush your lower ribs at the end of the stroke. Then push the handles down slightly to clear the blades from the water as you push them away from your body. Push "down and away." Keep your hands relaxed so the handles can roll along your fingers into the feathered position. Don't slouch at the finish. Keep your lower back firm and your upper back relaxed.

Recovery: Your hands lead between strokes. Push them away briskly from your body. Your arms should pull your upper body forward so that your shoulders are in front of your hips. Your wrists—which should remain flat as shown— should pass your knees before your knees rise. Notice that the blades are turned or feathered at the beginning of the recovery. As you start to roll up the slide, begin to square the blade for the next stroke. Notice that the blades stay very close to the water throughout the recovery.

Catch: The shins are nearly vertical. The blades are inches from the water. Complete the recovery with a slight lift of your arms to lock the blades in the water. Notice that the arms and back remain in the same extended position at the catch. Also notice that the fingertips are wrapped lightly around the oars and the wrists are flat.

Drive: The power portion of the stroke. Hang your weight from the oar handles. That means starting the drive with your legs, your strongest muscles, while holding your back and arms firm. As your legs approach full extension, lean back toward the bow and finally pull in with your arms.

KNOW WHERE YOU SHOULDN'T ROW

If you are new to a body of water, ask around to find out if there are any rules for rowers as well as any particular hazards to watch out for. On crowded rivers like the Charles (Boston) or the Schuylkill (Philadelphia), you are expected to row upstream on one side of the river and downstream on the other. You should know which arches of bridges you can row under and where the currents get squirrely. On tidal rivers or lagoons, find out where the rocks emerge first when the tide goes out. If you can, have someone who knows the water take you out and point out landmarks that you can use to plot your course. Eventually, you'll be able to row your course without looking around much at all. You'll learn to play the currents and the eddies to best advantage, where the deeper, faster water is, and where the reeds are just beneath the surface, ready to slow you down. You'll learn to curse novice rowers who cut you off. Maybe you'll even learn not to.

MAKING CONTACT WITH YOUR BOAT

When you next sit in your boat, notice that you have four points of contact that will determine how stable and how comfortable you are:

Your seat: Sit upright with your hips tilted forward so you feel your pelvic bones fall into the holes. Use those holes to make sure you are always seated squarely with your center of gravity over the center of the boat. If your pelvis is too wide, then you will need to modify your seat or find another one. Unfortunately, most boatbuilders make one width of seat, so you may have to shop around for other brands.

Your footstretchers: Whatever force you apply to your footstretchers, whether pushing off for a full power stroke or gently pulling yourself back up the slide during the recovery, the force should be equally distributed on both legs. Think of squatting down and leaping straight up into the air: You naturally apply the same amount of force with each leg. If you don't apply equal force, you'll leap to one side or the other. The same is true in a shell. If you don't apply equal pressure with your legs, you won't stay on course.

Notice that your footstretchers are adjustable fore and aft. If your footstretchers are set properly, your thumbs should brush the bottom of your rib cage at the end (release) of each stroke.

Whether your feet are secured by shoes or leather clogs, you should never tie them tight. If you find that your feet often come out of your footstretchers, then you are pulling too hard with them. In any case, you must be able to get out of your footstretchers immediately in case you flip.

Your hands: The last two points of contact, how you hold the oar handles, is probably the most important factor in rowing technique—that which separates hammers from technicians. Hammers wrap their fingers firmly around their oar handles and blister their thumbs against the ends. The tighter the grip, the more exaggerated and clumsy the rest of the stroke becomes. A tight-fisted rower tends to jam his blades into the water at the catch and rip them out at the release. Every random wave that hits the blade during the recovery throws a hammer off balance. There is a primal satisfaction to this struggle with the water. But it is not efficient.

Technicians allow their oar handles to float in their fingertips. The hands don't squeeze the handles, the fingers hook around them. The handles do not touch the palms at all. The thumbs press gently against the ends of the oar handles to keep the oars against the oarlocks. When the blades are "squared" (perpendicular to the water) during the drive, the wrists are flat, on a line between the knuckles and the forearms. To "feather" the blades (parallel to the water) at the end of the

stroke, the wrists bend slightly downward and the handles roll in the fingertips. The oars fall over in the oarlocks almost effortlessly. To square the blades at the end of the stroke the motion is reversed. The wrists rise slightly and the oar handles roll in the fingertips. If your grip is relaxed, your arms stay relaxed. Wakes or waves won't upset your balance. **REMEMBER:** Oar handles generally come in different sizes, so find a pair that fits your hands.

When you first begin to row, it will be very hard to maintain a light grip. You will instinctively grab your oar handles as if your life depends on it. You'll also try to rush into taking full strokes. That sort of enthusiasm will slow you down. Take your time and stay relaxed. If you have already done some sculling, but aren't sure you are doing it well, go back to the beginning and do these drills as if you had never sculled before.

FIRST STROKES

The Circle Drill

It's a lot easier to begin with a light grip on the oar handles if you start just rowing with one oar at a time. If possible, get someone to hold your boat at the dock while you practice. Otherwise, just row in circles. Sit back in the release position feeling your pelvic bones pressing into the seat and press your legs down (knees unlocked). Lean backward until your stomach muscles are just called into play. Hold one oar handle against the bottom of your ribs to keep your balance and begin to row with the other one.

At first just keep the blade squared perpendicular to the water and practice dropping it in with your arm extended, pulling through and pressing down to release it at the end of the stroke. As soon as you're comfortable, extend your stroke by leaning forward from the hips. When that feels good, practice feathering your oar at the release and squaring up again for the catch.

The Crossover

Before you can row with both oars at the same time you must deal with the problem known as the crossover. If your boat is properly rigged, your oar handles overlap by anywhere from 6 to 9″ when the oars are perpendicular to the hull. To solve this problem, most American boats are rigged so that the left hand crosses above and slightly behind the right hand. "Left over Right" is the standard jargon. The East Germans are rigged to "Right over Left." The choice is arbitrary, but it will be easier for you to stick to the American standard. If possible, have someone hold your boat so you can practice the crossover portion of the stroke, pulling your oars in and pushing them away. You'll understand why short fingernails help when you're starting out.

Arms Only—Shoulder Pick

Sit back in the release position with your legs straight, your oar handles pulled into your ribs, and your blades flat on the water. Hold your legs and body steady (not rigid) and begin to row just with your arms. Take one stroke at a time. Between strokes let your oar blades skim the surface of the water to keep you balanced. Practice feathering your oars with your fingertips: Let the blades roll into the square position just before you put them in the water for a stroke. At the end of the stroke, let the oar handles roll back and the blades fall flat against the

water. Practice for a few minutes just with your arms. You'll know you're ready for the next drill when you can complete an arms-only stroke without a death grip on the oar handles.

Arms and Back—"Swing Pick"

When you feel stable rowing with both arms, begin to use your body. From the release position, push your arms away from your body. Just before your arms are fully extended, bend forward from your hips to extend the stroke. Taking the stroke is just the reverse. Start to pull on the oars by swinging your body back and then finish the stroke by pulling in with your arms. To protect your lower back during the swing pick, don't "lock" your knees. Keep them just slightly flexed. Don't put a lot of pressure on the oars during the swing pick. This drill is to develop a fluid style, not power. When you feel relaxed with the swing pick (no death grip!), begin to add your legs and work up to a full stroke.

Adding Your Legs—"Quarter Slide" to "Full Slide"

The secret to adding your legs is to do it a bit at a time. From the release position, push your hands away, swing your body forward, and, as you approach full extension with your arms and back, break your knees and roll forward a few inches on the slide before dropping your blades in the water. Now you'll start pulling on the oars with your legs, followed by your back and finally your arms.

When you're comfortable using a little bit of the slide, add a little more. Gradually work on increasing the length of your stroke from quarter slide to half slide to three-quarter and then full. Once you can row at full slide, begin to work on raising your blades off the water on the recovery.

How long you take to reach a full stroke with your blades off the water depends on the water conditions, the stability of your boat, and how relaxed you can be. It may take hours or days or weeks. Take your time. If you try to rush it, you'll get tense, grip the oar handles too hard, and wind up with a hammer technique.

If you watch competitive scullers as they leave the dock, you often see them go through this same series of drills as a warmup. Each time you get in your boat, take a few minutes to reacquaint yourself with the water and become relaxed. Your hands are a good guide. You know you are warmed up when you can relax your grip.

Your first days on the water: In your first few days or weeks on the water, there is a paradox that you are going to have to acknowledge and overcome. It goes like this: Each rowing stroke is part of a continuous cycle. Your oars should be in constant motion without any pauses between one stroke and the next—like the bicycle chain going round and round.

But when you are learning to row, you will not be able to concentrate on the whole cycle at once. You will be forced to break up the stroke into manageable bits.

You can watch the paradox exert itself on different rowers in different ways. Some beginning rowers go for fluidity—doing everything wrong, but doing it gracefully. Other novices row like they swallowed the instruction book. They would look fine if you photographed them with a still camera.

How do you solve the paradox?   The key is not to try and fix everything at once. Each time you go out, your goal is to be fluid, to keep relaxed and easy in your stroke. But at the same time, each row should have its own focus—a particular portion of the stroke or technical consideration that you concentrate on. For your first few weeks, your focus should be fairly broad, such as working on your release, drive, or catch. If you change the focus of your workouts in a regular cycle, you'll be amazed at how much you improve each time you repeat a cycle. As you get more comfortable, your focus should become tighter.

THE MYSTERY OF THE BEGINNING . . .

They came forward easily and confidently and then, without any marked uplift of the hands or any marked display of energy in throwing back the body, in the twinkling of an eye the blade of the oar was covered to its full depth and instantly a mass of green water was piled up against it. For the rest of the stroke this solid-looking mass of water was swept back with unfaltering precision and at the finish the blade of the oar left the water as it had entered it, without flurry or splash, and the mass of water swirled away with scarcely a bubble round the edge of the vortex which the movement of the blade had set up.

Recovery: Your hands lead between strokes. Push them away from your body briskly. As you arms near full extension, lean forward from your hips. Once your arms are extended and you're leaning forward, bend your knees and roll your seat up the slide. Notice that the blade is turned or feathered at the beginning of the recovery. As you start to roll up the slide, begin to square the blade for the next stroke. Notice that the blades stay very close to the water throughout the recovery.

Catch: Your shins are nearly vertical. The blades are inches from the water. Complete the recovery with a slight lift of your arms to lock the blades in the water. Notice that the arms and back remain in the same extended position at the catch. Also notice that the fingertips are wrapped lightly around the oars.

Drive: During the power portion of the stroke "hang" your weight from the oar handles. That means starting the drive with your legs, while holding your back and arms firm. As your legs approach full extension, lean back toward the bow and finally pull in with your arms.

Release: Your oar handles should just brush your lower ribs at the end of the stroke. Then push the handles down slightly to clear the blades from the water as you push them away from your body. Push "down and away." Keep your hands relaxed so the handles can roll along your fingers into the feathered position. Don't slouch at the finish. Keep your lower back firm and your upper back relaxed.

TECHNIQUE DRILLS

Every experienced rower has a special sequence of drills either to help focus, relax, or simply get acquainted with the water. Below are some standard drills that you may find useful as part of your warmup, or any time that you need to focus.

Blades Square

This is a good drill for days when the water is flat and there is little wind. To develop a clean, quick finish to your stroke, practice rowing without feathering your blades during the recovery. Increase and decrease the stroke rate and pressure. You can make the drill easier by rowing half feather or quarter feather.

Pause Drills

To develop better balance and slide control, interrupt the recovery of each stroke with a brief pause. Start with a pause just as you release the blade; then, after a few strokes, pause with your arms extended (shoulder pick position); then with your arms and body extended; do it at quarter slide, half slide, and three-quarter slide. Pause for a second or two—just long enough to be very conscious of balance. Toward the end of the drill, insert a pause only on every third stroke.

Cutting the Cake

This drill is especially helpful for rowers who have not yet learned to start the recovery with their arms before their back and legs. At the finish position of each stroke, release the oar normally and extend the arms, but then pull the arms back to the release position once again before completing the recovery. This double arm action also teaches you to get your arms away quickly.

Rowing Blind

To improve your feel for the boat, close your eyes. Mentally break down your stroke as you row. Feel your body move smoothly up the slide. Listen for a perfect catch. When you open your eyes, note whether you drifted to port or starboard. As you improve, you should be able to maintain a straight course with your eyes closed.

Feet Out

This drill really feels awkward and silly, but it can come in handy. Simply untie your feet, rest them on the tops of your footstretchers, and row. It will help your recovery. It will also help prepare you for the time when your footstretchers break in the middle of a row.

A Skill and Drill Warmup

Shoulder pick (30 strokes)
Swing pick (30 strokes)
¼, ½, ¾ slide (30 strokes each)
½ pressure (30 strokes)
Blades square (30 strokes)
Pause drills (30 strokes)

Cool-down

Eyes shut (20 strokes)
Feet out of footstretchers (20 strokes)
Blades square (20 strokes)
Paddle easy (30 strokes)

Video Your Workouts

Even these days, coaches are hard to find, but you can improve a lot on your own if you can see what you're doing. Some people claim to learn by watching their shadows on the water, but that has never helped me. However, I have learned from watching myself on a video tape. If possible, have someone follow you in a launch and take close-up shots of the different phases of your stroke. You'll probably be able to diagnose plenty of problems just by watching yourself. You can also have a lot of laughs if you keep a video log of your progress.

If you get serious about technique, you can also buy videos of champion scullers for comparison. You can even mail your own video to one of several coaches who will assess your style and mail back suggestions.

THE LOOK OF CHAMPIONS

It is another paradox that as the oar enters the water, the speed of the hull is checked by the pressure exerted by the oarsmen on the stretcher and that the speed increases as the blades leave the water. So the boat should progress in a series of leaps, and most racing boats undoubtedly do progress in this fashion. Yet in all the crews I have had to do with that have developed exceptional speed, the boat does not travel by jumps, but holds its way so steadily that the variations in speed which must accompany the method of propulsion by oars are inappreciable to the eye.

A "Futt" or a "Cloop"

The major accent of the stroke, the sound made by the blade entering the water, should also be crisp and clean. If it is a squashy sound the beginning has been missed. . . . To my own ear it is best represented by the syllable futt, *given very sharply and decisively, but perhaps* cloop *represents it best for most ears. . . . Anyone who has heard and felt it in a first-class crew will not readily forget it. The trouble is that it is never heard but in a first-class crew, and first-class crews are rare. To my own ear [the oar leaving the water] sounds more like* chuf *than anything else. It should be a clean crisp sound. If it is too much of a swash it means that the blade has rowed light towards the end of the stroke.*

TO MEASURE YOUR PROGRESS, CHECK YOUR RUN

When you release the blade at the end of the strokes the pair of "puddles" of swirling water stay in about the same spot as the boat moves past. The larger the distance between these pairs of puddles, the faster you are rowing. The distance between puddles is the "run." Your goal is to put just a little more distance between puddles as you row to get just a little more run.

TO ROW WHERE YOU WANT TO GO

4

To V.
You're skilled at sculling, yet your skill
Is rather skill of hand than skill of skull.
The contents of your skull would scarcely fill
The hollow of the hand wherewith you pull.
But that, you'll say, is no fair test of mind
For larger hands, I own, you'll hardly find.
VIVIAN NICKALLS described in *The Ephemeral*, an Oxford magazine, c. 1890

In the beginning, paddling your single may seem a lot like traveling in a hot air balloon: It's a very satisfying way to go from point A to point B if you really don't care where point B turns out to be. You'll tour your body of water randomly. One blade will get stuck and spin you one way, and then the other will catch and spin you back. If you turn your head often to check your progress, you'll miss more strokes and your course will become even more erratic. Ideally, you have plenty of open water in which to wander. If you don't, you may find that trees or rocks appear unexpectedly. If yours is a popular rowing area, more experienced rowers will probably curse you whenever you fail to follow the prescribed traffic pattern. Forgive them. Stay relaxed. With practice your course will become more consistent and then you can worry about where you're heading.

Picking a "Point"

Your goal is to concentrate as much as possible on your rowing without having to look constantly over your shoulder. Before you begin to row, swivel around and scan the water. Decide where you want to go and check for obstacles, flotsam, or approaching traffic. Once you have chosen your course, point your bow in that direction and then sight directly down the stern of your boat and align yourself with an object on shore such as a tree or a telephone pole. Better still, find two objects, one behind the other, that form a straight line in the direction you want to go.

If you locate a point behind you and keep your stern aligned with it, you should not need to look over your shoulder very often. For the same reason, you should try to familiarize yourself with the major landmarks along the bank. For

Before you start to row on an unfamiliar body of water, ask around. If it is a popular rowing spot, find out the traffic patterns. Chances are someone has made a map of where you should row and where you shouldn't. Take it with you on your first trips.

open-water rowing, some rowers mount compasses on their shells.

Looking Over Your Shoulder

Novice rowers tend to finish one stroke, snap their heads around for a quick glance up ahead, and then go on to the next stroke. This is a mistake. Your head is very heavy—and the highest point off the water. Any sudden movement of your head will throw you off balance. Even worse, your boat is *least stable* when your blades are out of the water. The best way to look behind you is when your boat is stable—during the drive.

Begin to look behind you early in the drive. Swivel your head back in concert with your stroke. Keep your head upright and over the keel as much as possible and try to complete your scouting before you take your oars out of the water. If you work at it, you'll soon build an easy rhythm for looking around. Several quick glances in both directions over many strokes is much better than one boat-stopping turn-and-look.

Some rowers mount rearview mirrors to the gunnels of their boats or even to their eyeglasses or visors. I have never used a mirror, but it seems to help some people. One open-water racer I read about has had very good results with rearview mirrors. He says his only problem is that he often ends up on the wrong side of the things—such as the boat marking the finish line.

Steering

Shells are not like slalom kayaks. They are not designed to change direction rapidly, and they behave badly if you force them to. The key to a smooth course is to plan your turns well in advance. If you execute your turns gradually, you will not upset your balance or your rhythm.

The tendency of many scullers is to try to steer the boat by pulling harder with one arm or the other. In theory, this should work, but it doesn't—at least not when you're starting out. When you yank on one oar, you will tend to drive that blade deeper than the other. You will begin to turn in your desired direction at the beginning of the stroke, but then your blade gets stuck and you turn back again when you try to release the oar. It can be very frustrating—especially when every stroke you take seems to move you inexorably toward the edge of the dam.

The way to turn your boat successfully is to apply more pressure to one oar or the other using your legs. It's really very simple and it works very well. If you press down harder with one leg than the other, you'll make a steady, gradual turn.

If using your legs isn't turning you fast enough, reach out slightly farther with one arm and apply more pressure to that oar during the first half of the stroke. By the finish of the stroke, your application of power should be equal so that you can release the oars.

Panic Stops

The fastest stop I have ever witnessed was by a man on the Schuylkill who was just about to ram the nose of a beautiful wooden shell into the stern of a moored Boston Whaler. He was rowing at full

Looking Over Your Shoulder: When your blades are out of the water (and your boat is least stable) your eyes should be straight ahead. Right after you bury your blades at the catch, begin to turn your head in time with your stroke. Finish looking before you finish your stroke. In general, it is a lot less unsettling to take quick glances over several strokes than to try to see everything at once.

Panic Stops: If you practice in advance you will be able to stop almost immediately when you have to.

A rearview mirror mounted on your glasses or visor seems to help some rowers, but of course you end up looking around anyway.

power, at the catch of what would have been the fatal stroke, when a yell from the fisherman in the whaler and some sixth sense told him STOP. As far as I could see, the sculler let go of his starboard oar handle, grabbed for the water, and rolled out of the boat into the river. He was wet and looked a little foolish, but both boats were unscathed.

The more orthodox panic stop is at the finish of the stroke. Instead of pushing down to release your blades, leave them in the water at about half-feather, brace the handles against your body, and hold on. You can stop remarkably quickly with a little practice. Obviously, it is better to practice panic stops before you really need one.

Backing Down

Why you "back a boat down" I don't know, but it is easy to do. Notice that when some scullers row backward, they reverse the oars in the oarlocks. Reversing the oars makes your backing strokes more effective and it helps protect your oars. Wooden oars especially can be damaged if you apply pressure to the wrong face. The curved wood may be crushed and will then tend to rot.

Spinning Your Boat

To turn quickly, paddle with one arm and back-paddle with the other. It takes a few minutes to get coordinated, but when you do, you can spin your boat 180° without shifting your position at all.

LOOKING THE PART: CLOTHES AND EQUIPMENT FOR THE WELL-DRESSED ROWER

5

> I hardly care what I wear so long as it's tight. If it's baggy around the stomach, my hands get caught at the finish of the stroke. If it doesn't tuck in the back, it will get caught in the slide. JOHN BIGLOW, M.D.

You can row in anything. Some of the more formal British rowers of the late 1900s chose top hats and tails for men and flowered bonnets and flounced skirts for women. One of the less formal Yale men's crews of the mid-1970s occasionally stroked past the boathouse wearing nothing at all. These days when you go to a regatta you'll see clothes ranging from cut-off cotton sweatpants and tank tops to one-piece Lycra bodysuits. There are some performance differences to consider, but they don't matter that much. Whatever you choose to wear while rowing should be comfortable and suitable for the conditions, but, more importantly, it should be empowering. Such things as T-shirts are potent symbols. Choose yours accordingly.

In the college rowing tradition oarsmen (and occasionally oarswomen) bet their shirts on each race. At the finish line of the Harvard-Yale Boat Race, the

With a call to a rowing outfitter such as Boathouse Row Sports in Philadelphia, even a novice at the Craftsbury Sculling School can look like a veteran.

two crews pull their shells together and the losers strip off their shirts, hand them across to the winners, and then make the long paddle back to the dock naked to the waist. At most other collegiate regattas, the losers get to row back to the dock before handing over their shirts, but the result is equally poignant. Your racing shirt is your "lucky shirt." It stops being your lucky shirt when you lose. Then it becomes someone else's.

Outside of the collegiate circuit, racing shirts are rarely wagered but they are frequently traded. At the end of local races, competitors often gather to exchange T-shirts. At major international regattas, an elaborate bartering system has developed over the years where rowers swap for everything from rowing pins to shorts and even shells. You can sometimes tell a rower's complete history by the rowing clothes he has been issued or traded for. Even when rowers are nowhere near the water, they often wear some sort of symbol connected to rowing such as a T-shirt, a pin, or a hat. If you display your colors, you'll meet all sorts of interesting people.

When you begin to row, it can be very useful to collect a bunch of appropriate T-shirts and wear them around to attract other rowers. I know people who have found local rowing partners and coaches by wearing the right T-shirts. You can buy rowing shirts by mail from places like Boathouse Row Sports in Philadelphia (see Appendix III). And remember, when you buy a boat or an ergometer or go to a sculling school, buy their T-shirt. If you enter a regatta, you may want to make up your own racing shirt. One of my personal favorites was a shirt my teammates and I created for the U.S. National Team trials. We had been training in isolation for far too long. Our shirts had a silkscreen of a vulture with the words: PATIENCE MY ASS, I'M GOING TO KILL SOMETHING! It worked. If your first creation doesn't turn out to be lucky, trade it away.

A NOTE OF CAUTION: It is probably good for the sport that stores like The Gap occasionally have shirts with shells or rowers on them, but wearing them won't help you meet other rowers—unless yours is appropriately smeared with oar grease. In any case, beware of counterfeit racing shirts. These days it is possible to buy Harvard crew jerseys at various Boston boutiques. If someone gives you a real racing shirt, learn the story behind it and recount it with pride.

SUMMER ROWING

Power T-shirt: Make up something good.

Nylon shorts or "trow": The best rowing shorts look like cycling shorts without the cyclists' chamois in the crotch. Some rowing shorts have a larger pad sewn on the rear, which helps especially on long rows. If you wear loose shorts, such as running shorts, watch out for seams across the rear.

One-piece suit: A skintight one-piece suit will make you feel fast. They are very comfortable and you never have to worry about your T-shirt riding up your back. On the other hand, one-piece suits are more expensive, more difficult to care for, and harder to silkscreen.

Socks: If you have well-worn clogs, you may get away with bare feet, but start out with socks.

For warm weather, wear nylon rowing shorts and a tank top or, the ultimate in comfort, a one piece Lycra suit. Nike's Aquasox are terrific if you have to wade into the water. And don't forget a hat on a sunny day. Wear one that you can dip in the water to cool you off.

Hat: Keeps your brain from frying in hot weather. It's also nice to have one so that you can dip it in the water.

Aquasox: The best shoes for launching your shell, especially if you have to wade your boat into the water. If you have clogs mounted in your boat, you can wear your Aquasox as you row (made by Nike).

Wind shirt: The classic rower's Windbreaker is often not very well cut for either performance or comfort. They can billow like a windsock and yet can be constricting at the catch. Still, you'll probably want one because most other rowers wear them. Pullover Windbreakers designed for cyclists and skiers tend to be cut better, but you won't look like a rower.

WINTER LAYERING

Staying warm while rowing is often not a problem even in extremely cold weather. A more important question to consider is the temperature of the water. Once it becomes cold enough to warrant wearing layers of wool, you should prob-

The key to cold-weather rowing is layering. Wear wool or polypropylene tights and tops covered by a Windbreaker and a hat or wool cap.

Pogies slip over your oar handles to keep your hands warm on cold and windy mornings. The seat pad can save your rear on long rows.

ably not row alone. If you can't find a partner or a launch to follow, it is probably time to row only on your ergometer.

Top layers: To stay warm even when you're wet; the layer closest to your skin should be a soft, thin layer of either wool or polypropylene. Row Togs or LIFA polypropylene underwear work very well (unless you melt them in the dryer). If you wear cotton next to your skin, your sweat will chill you no matter what layers you have on top. Cotton works well as a second layer. If you become overheated, you can reverse the layers and put the cotton against your skin to cool down. Cover up with a wind shirt and a wool hat.

Bottoms: Your regular nylon or Lycra rowing shorts worn over a thin layer of polypropylene underwear is usually fine. In very cold weather, I prefer thick wool shorts. You'll appreciate them whenever a wave breaks in your lap.

Sweatpants: Wear them to warm up on shore, but take them off before you get in the boat. Wet sweats are no fun to row in.

Oar mittens or "pogies":   If you plan to row in cold weather you can save your fingers a lot of pain with a set of pogies. They are baggy hand covers with special holes to slip over the oar handles.

Assorted Extras

Gloves: Most rowers don't wear them. After a few days of rowing your bare hands will generally be tough enough to avoid blisters. But on some occasions— such as going to a rowing camp, entering a long race, or switching to saltwater— gloves can provide invaluable protection. The best gloves in my experience are thin leather golf gloves. Find a pair without any seams or stitching across the palms. After a long rest from training, I rowed the thirty-four miles Round Manhattan Race in golf gloves and didn't get a blister. Make sure you rinse your gloves after each workout. You may also want to oil them to keep the leather from cracking.

Seat cushion: If your seat is not comfortable, a seat pad may help. You can make your own out of a piece of soft foam such as ⅜″ Ensolite or you can buy one ready-made.

REMEMBER: If you use a pad, you may have to raise your oarlocks to adjust for the height of the pad (see Rigging, page 74).

Stroke counter: An onboard stroke counter like this Strokecoach from Nielsen-Kellerman can be a real boon if you are training by yourself. The device has a magnetic counter that mounts under your seat. The display tells you your strokes per minute and times your pieces. The problem with the device, at least for novices, is that it can make you worry about your stroke rating rather than how the boat moves.

The C.I.C. Pulse monitor (once marketed by Quantum XL and AMF) is one of the very few pulse devices that works, but it costs about $250.

The Strokecoach from Nielsen-Kellerman keeps track of your stroke rating, counts your strokes, and times your pieces.

6 THOUGHTS ON ROWING MACHINES

Over the last few years a new sport has emerged and is now spreading around the globe. It began, naturally enough, in Boston when CRASH-B (the Charles River Association of Sculling Has-Beens), organized the first World Indoor Rowing Championships on Concept II ergometers. The members of CRASH-B are former National Team rowers, and they were looking for an event to highlight their winter training. The result was an ergometer race, the chance to spend an awful lot of energy and emotion going absolutely nowhere, fast. With the help of Concept II they have managed to attract an ever-growing horde of competitors to the World Championships as well as spawn a series of regional competitions in boathouses and health clubs around the country. The Russians sent a team to Boston in 1988; a German won the event in 1989. Those who cannot make it to one of the regattas can "race" at home and send their scores to Concept II to be published in the annual World Ranking, but it's worth the trip to a regatta. A highlight of one recent World Championship was to watch two grandmothers duking it out in the finals. Their ergometers were connected electronically to a large video screen. Spectators sat on the bleachers and watched their "boats," bow ball on bow ball, sprinting madly toward the finish line. Age, it seems, does little to diminish the competitive spirit.

Before the Concept II erg, the only affordable machines for indoor rowing were the ubiquitous hydraulic rowing machines. Machines that mimicked the feel of real rowing cost thousands of dollars, took up lots of space, and were both noisy and cantankerous. Then Dick and Peter Dreissigacker at Concept II figured out that air resistance could feel very much like water resistance—spinning a fan could mimic pulling an oar. The first

The 1989 Indoor World Rowing Championships on the Concept II ergometer in Boston. M. Siejowski from West Germany is on his way to the world record time of 7:15.5 for 2,500 meters.

The Concept II ergometer (about $700) is rapidly becoming the world standard for indoor training. You can adjust the resistance on the Concept II in two ways: by switching from the larger to the smaller chain ring or by opening or closing the air vents on the side of the rotor. At first, just adjust the machine so that it feels comfortable. For best training, however, the machine should be adjusted so that the resistance on the machine matches the resistance in your shell. To do this accurately, have a friend time you with a stopwatch in your shell during the drive of the stroke (from the catch to the release) at full pressure. Then use the stopwatch to time the drive on your erg. Adjust the air vents so that the drive time is the same on your erg and in your shell. Make a mark on your erg so you can duplicate the setting.

Concept II ergometers harnessed a piece of "oar handle" to a bicycle wheel with plastic cards stuck in the spokes for air resistance and a bicycle speedometer to measure effort. Nowadays, the Concept II has a fancy aluminum fan and computer readout. The computer measures your work very consistently from one workout to the next and one machine to the next. You can hop onto a Concept II, row all-out for 2,500 meters, and know immediately how you compare to other rowers of your age and sex around the world. The only danger is of becoming an

Ergometron, a person who can thrash a machine but can't move a boat.

REMEMBER, *if you put an erg on the water, it sinks!*

Since the Concept II, several other machines have reached the market. Two quality ergs, the Coffey Ergometer and the Water Rower, have features that you may find more desirable than the Concept II. Calvin Coffey's ergometer (about $695) is similar to the Concept II, except that the fan is mounted below the seat. Coffey's most innovative machine, the Simulatoar (about $795), does a very good job of copying the full arc of a sculling stroke. The only problem is its "footprint." You'll need a lot of space.

The Water Rower actually uses water for resistance. When you pull on the handle, you spin a turbine through a tank of water. The more water you put in the tank, the more resistance you feel. It is an ingenious machine, made beautifully of cherry, and very quiet to row, but it costs about $1,800. The real problem with both the Water Rower and the Coffey Erg is that Concept II has become the standard. They are like Beta video machines in a VHS world.

If you bought one of the ubiquitous hydraulic rowing machines, don't feel badly. I have bought more than fifteen of them. When I was fitness editor at *American Health* magazine I had the opportunity to buy them for people in the office. Rowing on the hydraulic machine does not feel anything like rowing in a shell, but our art director had a hydraulic machine and lost twenty pounds by rowing every day for a couple of months. Anything that helped people to exercise seemed like a good thing to me. Anyway, I figured, how bad could a hydraulic machine be?

The immediate problem with the hydraulic machines was quality-control. Several of the machines, including one I shipped to my father in California and one that I transported to my brother in Morocco, were manufactured incorrectly and proved unrowable. Once we did get proper parts, however, the problems got more serious. Hydraulic machines, it turns out, were originally marketed as strengthening machines. When aerobics became popular they were repositioned in the marketplace—but the machines were not redesigned. If you use a hydraulic rowing machine as if it were a Soloflex (crank up the resistance and do three sets of 10 strokes), you'll probably be okay. If you try to row a hydraulic machine as if it were a shell, it is just a question of time before you hurt your back.

Fortunately, hydraulic machines are often too boring to be very dangerous. Few people use them for very long. I once sat on a plane next to the owner of the largest sporting goods retail store in New Jersey. Of the thousands of hydraulic rowers he had sold, not one had ever been returned with a part worn out. "It wouldn't take much rowing to break most of those machines," he said. "It tells you something."

Maintaining the Sensual Erg

Your goal is to have a lasting relationship with your ergometer as well as your shell. You want to bond with it—physically, mentally, and spiritually. You may need to develop a catalogue of fantasies to get through the bad pieces. It all takes time. On first encounter with your erg you are liable to get caught in the passion of the moment, go all the

When you don't want to erg alone, follow "The Rowing Machine Companion" home video. The 75-minute tape begins with a technique lesson by Stephen and Jinsey Kiesling. Then, thanks to a camera mounted in the bow of a quadruple scull and an eight, you row on the Charles with a member of the U.S. squad. Follow the video, stroke for stroke, through a choice of four separate workouts, beginning to advanced. Available by mail for $42.95 from The Rowing Machine Companion.

The Water Rower is a fine-looking machine with a frame of cherry wood. The resistance comes from a steel blade spinning in a gray Lexan tank. The more water your pour into the tank, the more resistance you feel. The major sound is the rush of water. It feels quite good .

way, and regret it. You'll wake up sore and dispirited. Instead, you must hold back. Stroke it gently on your first encounters. Become aware of how the machine moves and how your body responds. And leave after just a few minutes—well before you are spent. Each time you return, stay a little longer or add a little more pressure. Stroke long and low and keep a steady pace.

As you watch the pace monitor (min./500 m) you will discover a fundamental rule of stroking: *It's not the rate, it's the propulsion.* Rowing 30 strokes per minute is too high for a novice. Your strokes will be short and choppy. Instead, stay long and relaxed at 20 strokes per minute, or maybe 22. You'll probably find you can row at a higher pace (min./500 m) if you keep your stroke rate low. When I row on my erg, I don't pay any attention to my stroke rate. I am much more concerned with my pace through the water. In Chapter 12 you will learn about creating your own best fitness program on an ergometer and in a shell.

When you don't want to row alone, set your ergometer in front of your television and row along with The Rowing Machine Companion Home Video. This 75-minute video begins with a technique lesson on rowing machines from Jinsey and me. Then, thanks to a camera mounted in the bow seat of both a quadruple scull and an eight, you row on the Charles River with members of the U.S. National Team. Follow these champions, stroke for stroke, through a choice of four separate workouts from beginning to world class. It is available by mail from The Rowing Machine Companion.

7 GETTING COMFORTABLE: THE ART OF RIGGING

	Age	Height	Weight	Oar Length	Inboard	Span
John Biglow	33	6'3''	185	298 cm	88–89	158
Joe Bouscaren	34	6'2''	175	298 cm	87	158
John McGowan	54	6'4''	195	300 cm	88.5	161
Carol McGowan	52	5'7''	143	296 cm	88	158
Ginny Gilder	34	5'7''	145	296 cm	87	157
Ruth Kennedy	28	6'0''	130	298 cm	89	162

The Rig of Champions: The load or weight of each stroke is determined by the length of your oar, the inboard and the span between the pins. Here are examples of how different champion scullers rig their racing shells. You'll probably want your boat rigged "lighter" with a larger inboard and span. Experiment: A centimeter or two can make a large difference.

When my partner, Matthew Labine, and I ordered our shell for the Olympic trials in 1984, I assumed that it would arrive from West Germany ready to race. All we would have to do was bolt the riggers onto the hull, adjust our footstretchers, set the boat on the water, and start training. It was a foolish assumption. If you order a bicycle from a factory, you expect to receive the right frame size, but you would not expect it to arrive with the seat and handlebars already adjusted to your body. By the same token, when you buy a boat through the mail, you should expect to get the right hull size, but the movable parts—the oars, oarlocks, riggers, and footstretchers—will probably need to be adjusted to suit your body and rowing style. Matthew and I had always had a coach or a boatman to prepare our shells and they had given us the impression that "rigging" is black magic that takes years to comprehend. After all, a coach doesn't want his crews to worry about their equipment when they should be trying to pull hard. In fact, rigging is fairly easy to learn—and proper rigging can save you all sorts of pain and frustration. Unfortunately, Matthew and I didn't choose that path.

We should have realized that we would have a rigging problem when we picked up the boat at Kennedy Airport and unwound the bubble wrap that had protected the hull during shipping. The boat was almost completely assembled, but we could not figure out how to put our feet into it. After an hour or so of head-scratching we realized that the footstretcher supports had been installed upside down at the factory. We fixed that and tinkered with a couple of other minor problems, but we were left with a plastic bag full of odd bits of metal. It took several months to figure out that the extra parts could not possibly fit our boat and several years to muster the courage to throw the bag away. What really bothered me was that our boat came from Empacher—the company that then had the best reputation in the business.

Once we christened and launched our boat, it felt fine—at least at first. We had been off the water so long that anything would have felt good. After a few outings, however, we began to realize that we had problems: The boat felt as heavy as a log and almost as stable, but we blamed our technique and tried to adjust our bodies. Slowly we improved. Agonizingly slowly. We couldn't make the boat go straight, and once we did, we couldn't make it go fast. I developed tendonitis in one wrist because the oar was so hard to feather. I had a dream one night that we rowed across the finish line at the Olympic trials about a minute behind the winners. We saluted the judges' stand and then paddled ceremoniously over the dam.

About six weeks before the Olympic trials, we moved from New York to Philadelphia's Boathouse Row to join several other pairs who were training under coach Ted Nash at the Pennsylvania Athletic Club (Penn A.C.). We arrived at the boathouse late at night in the middle of a thunderstorm and slept in sleeping bags on the wooden floor. The Coke machine was out of Coke but offered several different kinds of beer, so our spirits were high—and remained that way for the next couple of days because the flotsam left from the storm was too thick to risk rowing in. When we finally did get out on the water, Ted watched us for about 10 strokes and then yelled through his megaphone,"I can see about 250 things you guys are doing wrong. If you

rig it right, that will take care of about 150 of them—and you'll then have a chance to fix the rest."

Ted roared off in his launch to gather the other boats from the first set of short races or "pieces"—probably the most humiliating pieces that I have ever rowed. We were left several boat lengths behind in every race.

The only thing that kept us from being completely dispirited was the faint hope that our dismal performance was not entirely due to our skill as oarsmen. When we got back to the dock we spent an hour with Ted getting a crash course in the art of rigging. Ted lowered Matthew's footstretchers—setting the heels of those size 16 shoes almost against the bottom of the hull so Matthew would be able to push off with his legs more effectively. Ted then pushed the oarlocks farther away from the hull to decrease the load on our oars and changed the angle or "pitch" that my oar blade hit the water so it wouldn't sink so deep. Ted said the pitch error was the cause of my tendonitis.

The effect was marvelous. The next time we practiced, we won a couple of pieces. More importantly, the correct rig allowed us to work on the last hundred things that Ted said were wrong with our technique. Ted declared that we would be able to fix 90 out of 100 by the trials. That would be enough to put us in contention.

Rigging seems complicated because what seem like small changes can make a great boat virtually unrowable. If your oar pitch is off by even a couple of degrees, for example, you will have difficulty maintaining your balance and keeping a straight course. Fortunately, if you have the right tools, basic rigging can be fairly easy and very satisfying. You can rig your boat according to some standard guidelines and then forget about it. Or, as you become a better sculler, you may want to experiment with your boat to get even more comfort, pleasure, and speed.

NOTE: Worrying about your rigging will slow you down.

WHAT YOU'LL NEED TO RIG

Notebook: Before you adjust anything, go through your rigging completely and measure everything first. Write down each measurement in your notebook. If this is your first time at rigging, close your notebook and measure everything again—just to make sure you are consistent. Later, when you adjust something, write it down as well. Good notes can save you all kinds of grief.

Shell owner's manual: If your boat must be adjusted outside the standard ranges outlined in this book, the owner's manual should give you more information.

Level ground: The light was better for photography on the dock, so we rigged it there, but you can go crazy trying to rig a boat on a small floating dock. Every footstep and wake will slosh your carpenter's level.

"Slings" or "trestles":   These are needed to support your boat. You can make your own out of wood or PVC tubing or buy camp stools.

Carpenter's level: It's nice to have a long (36") level, but you can get by with any accurate level and a straightedge.

Tape measure: Find one with both metric and American scales. If you can't do that, go completely metric.

Assorted wrenches: Protect your investment. Buy a box-end wrench to fit every nut and bolt on your riggers and footstretchers. An adjustable "crescent" wrench is a poor second choice that will sooner or later destroy your bolt heads. In any case, be gentle when tightening nuts and bolts.

Pliers: Use gently on tight wing nuts. Don't use pliers on other nuts or bolts.

Screwdrivers: For adjusting the buttons on your oars. You may also need a screwdriver to adjust your footstretchers. Make sure your screwdrivers fit your screws.

Pitch meter: If you don't have access to one, buy one. It is possible to adjust your oar pitch using a piece of string and a protractor, but life is too short. Either the Empacher pitch meter or the Pitchmaster are fine.

Tools of the trade: Don't forget your notebook.

Electrical (black) tape: Great for quick, temporary, fine-tuning of your pitch. Three layers (wraps) of black tape will change your pitch by 1°.

Shims: Wedges used to adjust the height of the oarlocks in older boats. In general, a shim that is 1 mm thick will raise or lower the oarlock by about 1 cm. Washers are good shims. So are the thin flat clips that secure a plastic bread bag.

Silver duct tape: Buy a big roll. You don't need it for rigging—at least I can't imagine why you would—but if you don't have a big roll handy, something will go wrong. I don't know why that's true, but it is.

FOOTSTRETCHER POSITION

The footstretchers should be set so that when you are at the finish of the stroke, legs down flat with your upper body leaning into the bow, your thumbs should just brush your shirt as you swing the handles past your body. If you are too close to the handles at the finish, you will not be able to swing them past your body. Your stroke will be short at the fin-ish and your release will be tight and cramped. If you are too far away from your handles, your reach will be short at the catch and you will have trouble with balance at the finish.

HEIGHT OF THE OARLOCKS

In theory, the height of the oarlocks is the distance from the bottom of the oar-locks to the waterline. In practice, height is measured from the bottom of the oarlocks to the lowest point on the seat. The height determines how much "clearance" you will have between the oar blades and the water as well as between the oar handles and your thighs. The ideal height of the oarlocks depends on the size of the hull, your weight, the size of your thighs, your skill and the water conditions. An experienced sculler rowing on flat water will keep his oarlocks as low as possible for the most efficient stroke. If you row on rough water or are just starting out, you'll want to allow yourself more room. The standard range is from 5½ to 7″ (14 to 18 cm).

A simple rule of thumbs: Set the height of your oarlocks so that at the finish of each stroke your thumbs just brush the bottom of your rib cage. That allows you a straight, efficient drive with enough room to release your oars at the finish of the stroke and clear the water on the recovery.

If your oarlocks are set too low, you may mash your knuckles on the gunnels at the catch of each stroke. At the finish of the stroke, your oar handles will be in your lap and you'll have no room to release the blades from the water.

If your oarlocks are set too high, you will tend to finish each stroke with the oar handles up at your chest or neck and will have a hard time keeping your blades in the water throughout the stroke. The boat will feel very unstable because the oars have too much room to flop around.

Allow for crossover: To allow room for your hands to pass each other at the crossover point, the left oarlock should be about 1 cm above the right oarlock.

Find a level place to work. A dock is not ideal if it wobbles when you walk on it.

To measure the height: Use your straightedge (carpenter's level) and tape measure. Lay the straightedge across both gunnels. Slide the seat below your straightedge and measure the distance from the lowest part of the seat to the bottom of the straightedge. Next measure from the bottom midpoint of each oarlock to the bottom of the straightedge. Add those two measurements together to get the height. (See drawing on page 82.)

Adjusting the height: Many new riggers have space for washers at the base of the tholepins under the oarlocks. The height of the oarlocks can be changed by adding or subtracting washers. Simply remove the nut at the tops of the oarlocks, slide the oarlocks off the pins, and then add or subtract washers.

On other boats, the only way to change the height is by using wedges or "shims" between the hull and the rigger. A shim on the bottom of the rigger plate raises the oarlocks. A shim on the top of the rigger plate lowers them. In general a shim that is 1 mm thick will raise or lower the height of the oarlocks by 1 cm.

HEIGHT OVER THE HEELS

The height over the heels is the distance from the lowest point of the seat to the lowest point of the heel cups. In many boats this height is not adjustable directly, but you should measure it anyway.

Let your knees be your guide: Sit in your boat at the catch position with your arms outstretched. If your heels are at the correct height, your shoulders should be above your knees so your arms can reach out comfortably to begin the stroke. You should be far enough forward on the slide so that your knees are directly over your ankles—your shins perpendicular to the water.

If your heels are too high, you will have trouble reaching over your knees. And

To measure the height of the oarlock, measure the distance from the seat to the bottom of the straightedge. Then measure from the bottom of the straightedge to the bottom midpoint of each oarlock. Add the two measurements together to find the height.

SHIM CAUTION: If you raise or lower your oarlocks by more than about 2 cm using shims, you may find that your oars get very quirky in the water. The blades dive at the beginning of the stroke and wash out at the end—or vice versa. Your problem is that the shims have changed what's called the lateral or outward pitch of your oarlocks.

To measure the height over the heels, measure the distance from the heel cup to the bottom of the straightedge. Then subtract the distance from the seat to the bottom of the straightedge (the first measurement you used to measure the height of the oarlock).

you won't be able to move far enough up the slide for your knees to be over your ankles. Your shins will be less than perpendicular. This problem is especially common in recreational boats, which tend to keep the seat low for stability. If you can't lower your heels, try raising your seat with a seat pad.

If your heels are too low, you'll tend to roll too far up the slide so that your knees are in front of your ankles. Your shins will be angled beyond the perpendicular.

To measure the height of your heels: Place the straightedge across the gunnels over the heel cups of your footstretchers. Measure the distance from the bottom of the straightedge to the bottom of the heel cups.

Move the straightedge over the seat. Measure from the bottom of the straightedge to the lowest point on the seat.

To calculate the height of the seat subtract your second measurement from the first. It should be 17 to 20 cm.

ANGLE OF FOOTSTRETCHERS

The angle of the footstretchers is the angle between the brace of the footboard and the horizontal. You can measure it with a protractor. Your goal is to be able to keep your heels down against the footstretchers throughout the stroke. However, when you are just starting out, you probably won't have enough flexibility in your ankles to achieve that goal if your footstretchers are set at the optimum angle—between 39 and 45°. When you come up to the catch of the stroke, your heels will rise out of the heel cups.

If the footstretcher angle is adjustable, you can decrease the angle to help keep

your heels in contact. It is better to set the footstretcher within the optimum range and then work on your ankle flexibility by doing warmup drills.

PITCH OR "STERN PITCH"

Your goal is to have your oar blades "set" naturally in the water so that the blades are fully covered when you pull on the oars. You should not have to spend any energy to keep the oars from diving too deep or washing out. If your oar blades were exactly perpendicular (90°) to the water when you dropped them in at the catch of the stroke, the blades would tend to sink too deep and throw you off balance. The solution is to tilt or pitch the blade slightly toward the stern. If you tilt the blade too much, it will tend to slip out of the water or "wash out."

Finding the best pitch involves some trial and error. The range is between 4 and 7°, with more experienced scullers tending to use less pitch. I prefer a pitch of about 5° with Concept II oars and 6° with wooden oars. Both blades must have the same pitch. If not, you will have a very difficult time maintaining your balance. If you can't maintain a straight course, check your pitches.

NOTE: Concept II makes some wonderful new oarlocks that allow you to accurately adjust your pitches without measuring tools. They are wonderful to row with.

"PITCHED" VS. "ZERO-PITCHED" OARS

Most American oars are made without any pitch, or "zero pitch." The blade is perpendicular to the surface of the button. All 4 to 7° of stern pitch is set at the oarlock. But some oars are made with a slight pitch built into the oar—usually about half the total desired pitch (2–3°).

There are complicated arguments for having some pitch in the oar and some in the lock. Most Europeans use pitched oars and most Americans now use zero pitch. I've never been able to feel any difference. The one real advantage of zero-pitched oars is that they can be used interchangeably on port or starboard. If your oars have pitch built in, your boat will be unrowable if you put the starboard oar in the port oarlock, or vice versa.

You should suspect that your oars are pitched if:

1. They are marked *Port* or *P* and *Starboard* or *S*.
2. If one oar has a *red* stripe (port) and the other a *green* stripe (starboard).
3. The club or college design on the oar blades may indicate port or starboard. For example, Yale oars are half blue and half white. The blue half is supposed to be on the bottom. If a port oar is being used starboard, the rower or coach can tell immediately because the blue is on top. These days, however, Yale oars tend to be zero pitch, so you sometimes see one oarman rowing blue side up. It looks funny, but it doesn't make any performance difference.

    If you suspect that your oars are pitched, test them directly with a pitch meter. You'll need a flat board about 1″ thick × 6″ long. Place the board on the floor. Set the oar face up so that the sleeve rests face up on the block at the button (where it would rest if it were in the oarlock). Have a friend press the back of the oar firmly against the block of wood.

    Place the pitch meter across the blade, base down about 20 cm from the tip. The pitch meter should be perpendicular to the shaft of the oar.

    If the bubble in the level remains centered, the oar has no built-in pitch. If the bubble is not centered, adjust the pointer until it is and read the pitch in degrees on the scale. Be careful to determine if the pitch is positive (oversquared) or negative (undersquared).

To zero the pitch meter, set the long metal pointer at 0° and then place the base along the washboard surrounding the cockpit. Hold the metal pointer at 0 and twist the plastic level until the bubble is centered. Now you are ready to test the pitch of your oarlock.

To measure the pitch in the lock, hold the pitch meter against the face of the lock. Adjust the level until the bubble is recentered and then read the pitch from the scale. This oarlock has only 4.5° of pitch (which explains why one oar was diving at the catch).

Measuring Pitch

Set your boat in slings and level it both fore and aft and from side to side. (You don't really need to level the boat fore and aft to use a pitch meter, but I'm superstitious, so I do.)

Zero the pitch meter: Set the long pointer at 0° and then set the base of it on the washboard of your boat. Hold the pointer at 0 and twist the level until the bubble is centered.

Measure the pitch at the lock: Make sure the oarlock is turned parallel to the keel. Press the pitch meter against the back of the lock as shown. Make sure the pitch meter is flush against the back of the oarlock.

Adjust the pointer until the bubble is centered again and read the pitch in degrees off the scale.

Measure the oars in the lock: In theory, if you have zero-pitch oars, you never need

To measure the actual pitch of the blade as it hits the water, first zero the pitch meter. Next have someone hold the oar in the oarlock and then measure the pitch against the blade. Measure the pitch of the oar in three positions: at the catch, with the blade perpendicular to the hull, and at the release.

to measure the actual pitch of the blades when the oars are in their locks. Whatever pitch is in the oarlock will be the pitch at the end of the blade. In reality, oars, especially wooden ones, tend to warp, so it's a good idea to check.

Level your boat and zero your pitch meter. Have a friend hold the oar firmly against the oarlock. Make sure the oarlock is parallel to the keel (the oar is perpendicular to the keel) and the oar handle is about 14 cm above the seat. To measure the pitch, hold the pitch meter against the oar blade about 20 cm from the tip and perpendicular to the ground.

A fast, temporary way to fine-tune your pitch is with wraps of electrical tape around the face of the oarlock. If you wrap the tape toward the top of the pin, it will increase the pitch. If you wrap the tape toward the bottom, it will decrease the pitch. Three wraps of tape is equal to about 1°. If you use more than five wraps, chances are the tape will slip and you will create a mess.

OUTWARD OR "LATERAL PITCH"

If you think about it for a moment, you will realize that the ideal stern pitch of the blade is not the same throughout the stroke. At the catch you would want a little extra tilt (say 7½°) to prevent your blade from going too deep. But at the release of the stroke, you would want less pitch (perhaps only 4½°) so the oar will be easier to take out of the water. There is a way to do it. In fact, it may already be built into your boat. It's called outward or lateral pitch—the tilt of the tholepin (not the face of the oarlock) away from the shell. Generally, lateral pitch is not something you need to worry about. With most riggers you can't adjust it. But you should understand it.

If there is zero lateral pitch set in your tholepins, your blades will maintain the same stern pitch throughout the stroke. It will be 6° at the catch, midway through the drive, and at the release. But if your pins are tilted outward at 1°, your stern pitch will vary from about 7½° at the catch to 6° in the middle and 4½° at the release. If the pin is tilted at 2°, you'll get even more variation—from about 9° at the catch to about 3° at the release. You would never want to have more than 2° of outward pitch.

To measure lateral pitch, make sure the boat is level from side to side. Zero your pitch meter by laying it across the tracks rather than along the gunnel. With the pitch meter perpendicular to the keel,

To measure outward or lateral pitch, first zero the pitch meter across the tracks of the slide. With the pitch meter perpendicular to the hull, hold it against the tholepin (not the face of the oarlock) and center the bubble again. The lateral pitch of this oarlock is almost 2°. *It is essential that the pin does not lean fore or aft—if it does, that will alter the pitch through the stroke.*

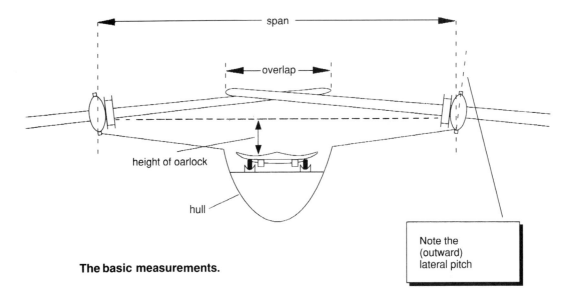

span

overlap

height of oarlock

hull

Note the (outward) lateral pitch

The basic measurements.

hold it against the pin (not against the oarlock).

Another way is to measure the stern pitch of the oar blades at the catch and finish of the stroke. If the stern pitch remains in a reasonable range—and both sides are the same—then you don't need to worry about the lateral pitch.

POTENTIAL DISASTERS WITH LATERAL PITCH

Negative pitch: If your pin tilts inward—toward the hull—rather than outward, you have what's called negative lateral pitch and your blade won't set well at the catch and will then stick at the finish. This should not happen, but I have seen it occur as a result of:

1. Mistakes by the boatbuilder
2. Collisions that bent the rigger
3. Using too many shims to raise the riggers

REMEMBER: If you raise or lower the height of your oarlock by using shims between the rigger and the hull, you will change the lateral pitch. In general, raising or lowering your oarlock by 1 cm will change your lateral pitch by 1°. Shimming your boat up by more than a couple of centimeters can make your boat virtually unrowable unless you adjust the lateral pitch accordingly.

SETTING THE "LOAD" OR WEIGHT OF THE STROKE

You may notice if you switch from one shell to another that one boat feels lighter during the stroke than another. It's somewhat the same sensation as changing gears on a bicycle. One boat feels like it's set in first gear (the "load" is light so you can row at a very high cadence). The other boat feels as if it's in tenth gear (each stroke is slow and powerful). In an ideal scull, you would be able to change "gears" as easily in a shell as on a bike. You might warm up in one gear and race in another. If you were slogging into a headwind or the current, you would shift into a lighter gear. If you had the wind or the current helping you along, you would shift into a heavier gear.

In fact, you *can* adjust the "gearing" on most shells, but you *can't* change that gearing once you are on the water. Virtually all recreational scullers and most racers are content to adjust the gearing to an average feels-pretty-good position and then never fool with it again. Other rowers adjust their gearing according to the wind, the current, the training season, or even their moods. In general, you want to find a load in which, at a comfortable stroke rating, you spend twice as much time on the recovery as the drive. Your recovery-to-drive ratio should be about 2:1.

The load that you feel during the stroke is determined for the most part by how far the blades arc through the water on each stroke. If the blades travel through a long arc, the load feels heavy. If they travel through a short arc, the load is light. The length of the arc depends on two major factors: the "span," the distance between the two oarlock pins, and the "inboard," the placement of the collar on the oar.

Let's say the load on your oar handles is too heavy, that you slog through each stroke and can't sustain a steady rhythm. To lighten the load, you could either increase the span between your tholepins or increase the inboard on your oars—or a little of each. Since the span is the most difficult to change, your best bet is to set

it more or less right and then do all your fine-tuning with the inboard of your oars.

SPAN BETWEEN THE THOLEPINS

The most dramatic way to change gears is to alter the span: the two oars are levers; the two pins are fulcrums. The

The span is the distance from one tholepin to the other. You also must make sure that each pin is the same distance from the center of the cockpit.

closer the pins are to the boat, the less leverage you have and the heavier the stroke. If you push the pins farther away from the hull, you have more leverage and the load feels lighter. Another way to think of the load is in terms of the arcs that the blades move through during the stroke. If the pins are moved closer to the boat, the blades travel through longer arcs and the load is heavier. If the pins are pushed away from the boat, the arcs are shorter and the boat feels lighter.

To find the span, measure from the center of one pin to the center of the other. The only difficulty is that both pins must be the same distance from the center of the boat. In other words, the "spread" should be the same. Otherwise, the leverage of one oar will be different—it will feel lighter than the other one and you will tend to row in circles.

To make sure the pins are evenly spaced from the center of the hull, measure the width of the hull from gunnel to gunnel directly in line with the tholepins. Divide that number by two to find the distance from the edge of the gunnel to the center of the boat. Hold this number on your tape measure at the outer edge of the gunnel and extend your measuring tape out to the center of the pin. The number on the tape at the centerline of the pin is the spread. The spread to each oarlock should be exactly one half the span.

When you move the span even slightly, you will notice a large change in the gearing of your boat. The spread ranges from 60 to 65" (152 to 165 cm); the bigger and stronger you are, the smaller your spread should be.

INBOARD: ADJUSTING THE OAR BUTTONS OR "COLLARS"

The oars have a ring or collar that clamps around the shaft and fits against the oarlock. Its purpose is to keep the oar at the right position against the oarlock. Another way to change the load or gearing of your boat is to move the collars. Like changing the span, moving the collars is a way of moving the fulcrum of each oar.

If you move the collars out toward the blades, the arcs the blades travel through get smaller and so the load gets lighter. If you move the collars in toward the handles the arcs grow larger and the load gets heavier. Moving the collars is a

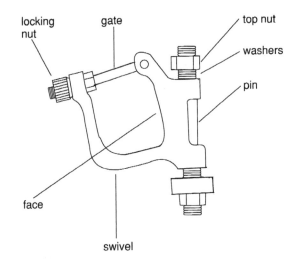

simple operation with a screwdriver. Just loosen each screw and slide the collar. By convention, the distance you should consider when you adjust the collar is the "inboard," the distance from the working side or face of each collar to the ends of the oar handles. Most oars range from 9' 8" to 9' 11" (296 to 302 cm) and inboard measurements range from 33 to 35" (84 to 90 cm).

Oar Handle Overlap

If you have set the spread and the inboard correctly, the oar handles should overlap 7–9" (18–22 cm) when the oars are perpendicular to the boat. If the overlap does not fit into this range, something else has probably gone wrong. Check your other measurements.

WORK THROUGH THE PIN

This final measurement causes all sorts of confusion. No two people explain it the same way, but it can be useful if for no other reason than as a check to ensure that everything else is right.

1. Sit in your shell at the dock and roll

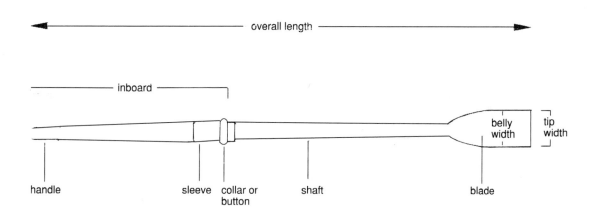

forward all the way to the catch position with one blade in the water as if you were going to take a stroke. Use a felt-tip pen to mark the position of the center of your seat (in line with the two holes in your seat) on your slide.

2. Get out of the boat and check your felt-pen mark in relation to the tholepins. If you want, take a piece of string and tie it between the two pins on your oarlocks. When you rolled your seat up to the catch, did the seat go beyond (through) the line of the pins?

If your mark is exactly in line with the pins (along the string), the distance through the pin is 0. If your seat moved 1″ beyond the line of the pins, the distance is 1″. In a single scull the standard range is between 0 and 2″ through the pin.

Why Should You Care about the Work-Through?

Increasing the work through the pins will move the stroke toward the bow; it will increase the catch angle and decrease the finish angle. Decreasing the work-through will move the stroke toward the stern; it will decrease the catch angle and increase the finish angle.

Fiddling for More Comfort and Speed

As you become more experienced, you will probably start to fiddle with your rigging in the hope of making your boat more comfortable, faster, or both. When you do fiddle with your rig, be conservative. Unless the rigging is completely messed up, change only one thing at a time, and only a little bit at a time. A large change can lead to confusion and/or injury. Make sure you record in your notebook any changes you make—as well as how you feel about the change. Your rigging will slip occasionally—you'll bump something just before you plan to start a long row or a race. If you have good records, you'll be rowing comfortably again in a few minutes. If you don't have records, who knows?

8 PULLING TOGETHER: THE CRAFTSBURY SCULLING SCHOOL

During the first three years of our marriage, Jinsey had only once worked out on my rowing ergometer—and that suited me just fine. We shared other sports together: tennis, volleyball, and even canoeing. But rowing was different. Very different. Some men make a ritual of bowling, jogging together, or watching football. For me it's rowing; when I can't get into my shell, I get on my ergometer and imagine that I'm on the water. Jinsey had thought it best to remain a casual observer of that part of my life, but it was early summer, our nerves were frayed from too much city, and we were desperate for a vacation. Jinsey needed to relax in the country and I needed to row, so we found ourselves driving north toward Vermont for a week in the country at the Craftsbury Sculling School. We shared a wonderful sense of adventure mixed with a profound sense of dread.

"This won't be the end of our marriage?" Jinsey asked me, only half joking.

"No, it will be fun."

"Maybe we should row together so we can use your boat when we get home."

"*That* will be the end of our marriage."

The Craftsbury Sculling School is in the rugged "northeast kingdom" of Vermont, only a few miles from the Canadian border. It's a long drive from anywhere, but the journey has become a pilgrimage for would-be scullers of all ages. "Sweep" rowers (one oar per person) go to learn the art of two-oared sculling. Beginning recreational scullers go to become comfortable on the water and to learn proper technique. Advanced rowers go there for a vacation with unlimited rowing on flat water.

As we got closer to the camp we began to talk about it seriously for the first time. Jinsey worried that she would embarrass herself: She would be forced into a pencil-thin racing single and it would flip over at the dock. But she seemed even more uncomfortable by the thought that she might *enjoy* rowing and that it would become a source of tension between us. I said that I didn't understand her concern, but I did.

If Jinsey didn't discover that she loved to row, if she didn't appreciate it, I would be very disappointed. But for her to love rowing might be worse. The real magic of rowing for me is to have my strength perfectly matched and amplified by as many as seven other oarsmen in a shell so that each of us feels the power of the entire crew. A poorly matched crew saps everyone's strength and makes a boat wallow.

When we arrived at Craftsbury we found that the accommodations were not deluxe, just dorm rooms with single beds and communal bathrooms. The dining hall, where the rest of the group had already gathered for orientation, was casual—a place where you could feel comfortable wearing rowing shorts and a sweaty T-shirt. Other than the lake and the boathouse, there was not much else at Craftsbury, and both of us felt a little disappointed. I had forgotten the pure mindless luxury of having nothing to do all day but make a circuit from my room to the boathouse to the dining hall, a

The Craftsbury Sculling School is a summer camp for kids up to age 80. There's not much to do but row, eat, and sleep, but that seems enough for a great vacation.

cycle interrupted only by mountain-bike rides through the woods or an occasional trip to the drive-in for ice cream.

A few minutes after the orientation meeting, the first lesson began—and fulfilled Jinsey's vision completely. The exercise was to climb into a narrow-hulled intermediate-level single, push away from the dock, and flip over. It was more difficult than it seems. Even a narrow boat is fairly stable, so long as you keep a grip on both oar handles. Once you let go, however, turning upside down comes naturally. Fortunately, the water of Hosmer Lake is clean and, in July, fairly warm. Climbing back into the boat is easier than it looks, and for the moment Jinsey's nervousness vanished. We were each assigned to boats for the week and then we paddled up and down the lake for about an hour to get the feel of the water. When we walked back up the trail toward dinner, Jinsey's eyes were shining. "I like the time between strokes," she said. "The glide. It's like swimming."

Over the next few days I began sculling with a vengeance, trying to build up to "full pressure" as quickly as I could. My initial goal was three consecutive full-pressure strokes without getting my oar blades stuck in the water. Then I built up to five, then ten, then twenty. The afternoon of the third day of camp I went out to time myself down the length of the lake, about a mile and a half. It had just rained and the water was flat and the air was still. I was completely alone on the lake, wearing a faded Olympic Team T-shirt. I paddled well away from shore, aligned my boat down the lake, and called to myself in French the starting commands used in an international regatta. It was on the second stroke or

maybe the third that my boat tipped slightly to one side and I saw to my chagrin that I had not secured the gate or "keeper" on the top of that oarlock. The oar popped out of the lock and in an instant I was in the lake, upside down. As I floated beside my shell in the middle of the lake I swore at my own stupidity—until I noticed that the water felt wonderful. Maybe I didn't really need to know how fast I could row the length of the lake. Then I began to laugh—harder than I'd laughed in a long time.

Jinsey was having adventures of her own. With my encouragement she tried to switch too soon into a narrow boat and capsized several times. Each time she turned over, she got more frustrated and less stable. She returned to her wide-bottomed boat and vowed to take her time. For the next couple of days she paddled happily alongside other first-time scullers who were almost twice her age. When she began to extend herself again and pick up more speed, I noticed that she had managed to avoid a couple of technique problems that had plagued my rowing for a decade.

That night the group gathered to watch videos of several world-class scullers. I was less than enthusiastic, but Jinsey was attentive. "Pretty blade work!" she gasped at one point. Thanks to all the coaching and frequent videotape sessions, Jinsey was not only rowing well, she was developing a sophisticated eye for the sport. Maybe we should try rowing together.

It was the last full day of camp when Jinsey and I finally carried the long, slender Vespoli "double" scull down to the dock. The last people to row in the boat had been training for the U.S. National Team trials, so the rigging was unforgiv-

The author and photographer taking a break between rows.

ing, ready to race. This is going to be a disaster, I thought to myself.

I had assumed that I would set the pace in the "stroke" seat, allowing my 215-pound body to create a steady rhythm up and back on the sliding seat for Jinsey to follow. Instead, she wanted to set the stroke. I had to follow her, to match every movement she made exactly. Suddenly I felt like the novice, large and lumbering, falling off tempo on a beat that seemed unfairly delicate.

"Stop rushing the slide," she snapped back at me over her shoulder with the authority of a veteran. "Relax!"

Finally, I did relax, and for a few strokes that day the two of us rowed as one and the only sad part was that the light was fading and we had to return to the dock.

9 STAY LOOSE, STAY HEALTHY!

One of the traditional rituals at many rowing clubs is the pre-workout stretch, which earlier in my career I understood to mean the pre-workout nap. I would lie on the ground, put my hands behind my head, and doze off until I was ready to launch. Stretching seemed uncomfortable and unsatisfying, so I didn't do it. If anyone asked me about stretching, I replied that rowing kept me flexible—or at least it kept me flexible enough for rowing. That is not true. When I watch old videos of my rowing, I can see the signs of poor flexibility. I can feel them now.

I first began to worry about flexibility when I was tested at a Manhattan one-on-one fitness center not long after the 1980 Olympic Team split up. The results were not too encouraging:

Shoulders	Normal mobility
Upper back	Hypermobile
Lower back	Hypomobile
Hip flexors	Hypomobile
Quadriceps	Hypomobile
Hamstrings	Hypomobile

It took me a few moments to remember that "hypo" means "less than" and that my best years of training had left me less than mobile—at least below my belly button. More recently, I was at a doctor's office staring at an X-ray, seeing my vertebrae for the first time. I had a lower backache that wouldn't go away. The immediate cause of the ache was diving for a volleyball, but I knew that wasn't the underlying problem. As it turned out, one vertebra—the hinge between my legs and torso for the millions of strokes I rowed—was worn down to half its original size. As I looked at the X-ray, each treasured rowing memory was suddenly undercut with this new picture of my spine: stroke after stroke, slowly, painlessly, grinding away. The doctor's explanation was clear. "You don't stretch much, do you?" he said. "It looks like it's time for you to start."

Now I stretch for a few minutes almost every day. When I don't, my back lets me know. So long as I listen to my back I can row. But I do wish I had started stretching a long time ago.

On the other extreme, I know several rowers who happily contort themselves for half an hour of stretching before *and* after each workout. I think they are wasting their time. Most of us need a little more flexibility than we have, but much less than stretching zealots would have us believe. Stretching is a poorly researched area of fitness science. But the work that has been done indicates that a little stretching goes a long way— and that you can overdo it. The rule of thumb here is that if you enjoy stretching, and do it often, chances are you don't need to push for more flexibility. If you hate to stretch, then you probably need to spend more time at it. In other words, the wrong people tend to stretch.

Stretching Self-Test for Minimum Flexibility

There are two simple tests to see if lack of flexibility is hurting your rowing. Before you try them, warm up your muscles by paddling for a few minutes on your ergometer or in your shell.

Finish flexibility: From the finish position, you should be able to tilt your body forward from your hips *before* your slide moves. If you can't, your hamstrings are too tight. You'll tend to slouch at the finish of the stroke and have trouble releasing your blades from the water. Ignore this test at your peril! You may be on your way to lower-back problems. As Bogart said: "Maybe not today or tomorrow, but soon and for the rest of your life."

Catch flexibility: You should be able to move *slowly and easily* up to full compression (shins perpendicular to the water) at the catch while keeping your heels close to the footstretchers. If you have to "go ballistic" to reach full compression, or if your heels can't stay near the stretchers, your calves and Achilles tendons are too tight. As you row, you'll probably notice that your shell slows down dramatically just before the catch of each stroke and that the stern bounces up and down a lot. Lack of flexibility is making you push against the footstretchers before you reach the catch.

If you don't pass the tests, you'll have a wonderful opportunity to improve your rowing just by stretching. Even if you do pass the tests, you still may need to stretch to keep your muscles limber as you get stronger. Here are some guidelines to help you get the most out of whatever time you choose to spend stretching.

RULES OF THUMB FOR STRETCHING

Never stretch a cold muscle. Always warm up before you stretch. For long-term flexibility gains, the best time to stretch is *after* you exercise.

When you stretch, listen to your body. Set an even, deliberate pace that allows you to focus on the muscle group you're working. Push only until you begin to feel the muscle—not to the point of discomfort—and hold for 20 to 30 seconds.

Pain means *no* gain. If it hurts when you stretch, you're pushing too far. You trigger a protective reflex in the muscle, the "stretch reflex," that will leave you less flexible.

Stretch very slowly and stay relaxed. Concentrate on breathing slowly and deeply. Time your stretches by counting your breaths.

Don't expect sudden changes. Nature uses the calendar, not the clock, to time flexibility gains.

Quadriceps Stretch

Stand facing a wall. Lean against it with your right hand. Grab your ankle with your left hand and tuck your heel into your rear. Hold for ten breaths, making sure that your knees are together and that you're not leaning off to one side. Repeat on the other leg.

Achilles Stretch

Put both hands on the wall. Place your right foot about 12 to 18″ behind your left, making sure both feet are parallel. Lean forward and bend both knees, making sure that your right heel stays on the ground. Hold for ten breaths and switch legs.

Still leaning against the wall, extend your left foot another 12 to 18″. Your left leg should be almost straight behind you with your knee and toes on the ground. Lean forward from the hips, keeping your torso erect. Make sure your right foot stays flat against the ground. Hold for ten breaths, then switch legs.

Hurdlers Stretch

Sit on the floor. Extend one leg straight out in front of you and draw the other leg up so that your knee points away from you and the heel of your foot is pressed against the inner thigh of your extended leg. Bend from your hips, drawing your upper body closer to your extended leg. Hold 15 seconds and reverse legs.

Look Away

Sit on the floor. Extend one leg straight out. Cross your other leg over the extended leg, placing your foot on the floor. Turn your upper body away from the extended leg. Hold ten breaths. Repeat with the other leg.

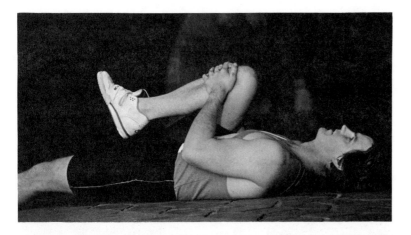

Hamstring Raises

Lie on your back with your knees bent and your feet flat on the floor. Gently grab your left leg behind your knee and pull it toward your chest. Then slowly straighten the leg up toward the ceiling. Circle your foot four times clockwise and four times counterclockwise. Relax the leg, pulling the knee gently toward your chest. Lower the left leg back to the starting position and start with the right.

Trunk Curls

The final part of your stretching routine should include strengthening exercises for the abdominal muscles to help balance the work you do with your back. For trunk curls, keep your legs loose and relaxed. Fold your arms across your chest and curl your trunk up—one vertebra at a time. Hold for a moment and then curl back down. (Build to three sets of twenty repetitions.)

Cross Training—Race Walk to the Dock

Oddly enough, one of the best stretching exercises for rowing is race walking. Race walking loosens up your hips, tightens your lower abdominals, and stretches your ankles and hamstrings. The technique may still look strange in public in your part of the country, but it really helps. For flexibility, race walking to the boathouse before practice makes a lot more sense than jogging. The only better activity for stretching is low-impact aerobics.

FIRST AID

10

You never know what is enough unless you know
what is more than enough.—William Blake

Every couple of years a rower drowns—usually a person sculling alone in the dark, in very cold water, or flood conditions, one who capsizes and tries to swim for it. Occasionally a rower is killed by a powerboat. Aside from these rare tragedies, rowing is a relatively safe sport. If your rowing goals are fitness and health, rowing should never be painful. If it hurts, you are pulling harder than you have to. However, if you get caught up in the sport and want to compete—as in any sport—you risk becoming a victim of your own enthusiasm. You may push too hard, too fast, and strain something.

Probably the most dangerous myth in sports is that great athletes "play with pain." If you play with pain, or try to ignore it, you will get hurt. It's that simple. The best athletes have to work with some pain as they train—just like working with any other sensory information.

They learn to understand the language of their muscles, monitoring all their sensations like the needle on a tachometer. In technical words, when trained athletes push harder, they associate rather than disassociate themselves from their bodies. By coddling pain, keeping it close, they keep it down to the level of sensory information, stripping it of the fear and uncertainty that might make it overwhelming. Any time they feel something different, a new pain, they slow down and figure out what's going on.

There are simple rules that can help you to become an associator and avoid injury no matter how high your goals.

■ Start slowly. With each new activity you have to learn a new language from your muscles. No matter how good you feel, do less than you think you can for at least the first few days. Stop long before anything hurts. The high of a new sport can be glorious, but it can lead you to overextend yourself.

- When you're ready to push harder, stay focused on everything your muscles are telling you. With every new sensation, ask yourself if you would mind feeling the same way the next time out. If you would rather not, ease off. Most injuries of the chronic low-grade type will stop hurting about 10 minutes into a workout. If you feel the pain increasing during a workout, you've got a problem. Stop what you are doing and rest for at least three days. This would also be a good time for you to schedule a trip to the doctor to get an accurate diagnosis and possible treatment.
- Any pain, tenderness, or nagging soreness or stiffness left over from one workout to the next means that you should cut your workout program in half—and eliminate high-intensity workouts.
- Don't let competition fool you. Adrenalin, endorphins, and a host of other chemicals charge you up and numb your pain sensors. A good rule of thumb is never to race harder than you practice. If you haven't pushed that hard in training, don't try it in a race. Your goal, after all, is energy and performance—not to see how much punishment your body can take.

IF YOU DO STRAIN SOMETHING

The moment of injury is in a way the beginning of a rather odd race—modern sports medicine vs. your body's natural protection system. If your body immobilizes the injury before you do, it can cost you a lot of extra time and discomfort. When you get injured, blood rushes to the site. The blood cells swell, slowing down circulation. That swelling helps protect the injury, but the loss of circulation can also mean that the injury will take longer to heal and your original flexibility may never return.

If you think you may have suffered a muscle, tendon, or ligament strain or sprain, don't keep rowing to find out. Minutes wasted early can cost you weeks of extra discomfort. The best advice is RICE (Rest, Ice, Compression, and Elevation). You can do all four on the way to your physician.

All told, most musculoskeletal injuries will take about six weeks to heal completely, if you give them a chance. In the meantime, you can often maintain your conditioning by switching sports. But if you try to get back to your old activity too soon, you can count on another six weeks of injury—and maybe another six weeks after that.

ROWING NUISANCES

Blisters: Early in my sister's freshman year at Yale when, like many novice rowers, she had a handful of nasty blisters, she went to the movies with a shy young man who finally got up the nerve to reach for her hand and give it an affectionate squeeze. She screamed. The relationship never recovered.

The first line of defense against blisters is to increase your rowing gradually. Second, have oar handles that fit your hands and keep them clean. Rinse the handles after each row. Every week or so, scrub them clean with a bristle brush and soap.

If you do get a blister, use a small sharp scissors to cut a tiny hole out of the middle of the bubble. Drain the blister and press the remaining skin back down. With any luck, the old blister will "take" and become the top of a new callus. In any case, keep the blister clean with soap and water and keep it pliable with Vaseline or an antibiotic cream like Neosporin. If the liquid inside the blister has pus in it, head for your doctor.

To protect your blisters while you row, the high-tech solution is a Spenco Blister Kit, which contains Spenco's "2nd Skin"; this is a gel sheeting that has the feel and consistency of human skin. It works well to reduce friction over a blister and make rowing pain-free. First lubricate the blister with Neosporin and then cover it with 2nd Skin. Finally, secure it with Spenco Adhesive Knit or athletic tape.

If you row properly with your oar handles in your fingertips, you should not get blisters on your palms. If you do, you've got a problem. Wrapping athletic tape horizontally around your hand will almost invariably create more blisters than you started with. You may have some success using a combination of 2nd Skin and Adhesive Knit covered with a golf glove. Better still, go bare. The discomfort in your palms will cause you to row properly with your fingertips.

Warts: If you notice a wart developing on your hand, take immediate action with a do-it-yourself wart medicine or a trip to the doctor. One wart and a sweaty oar handle can create a handful of nasty growths for yourself and whoever else happens to use your oar. If you have warts, wash your oar handles after use.

Cramps: "There's nothing quite like hopping on one leg and trying to massage the cramp in the other, especially in the middle of the night," one masters rower told me. He said his legs tended to cramp after he pushed beyond a certain low level of rowing. He demonstrated his hopping and rubbing technique, but it didn't look promising.

Whenever you increase the amount of exercise you do, your muscle cells are damaged. For some people, cramps seem to be a by-product of the repair process. The best way to avoid cramps is to lubricate the recovery process by drinking plenty of water. Hard exercise followed by diuretics such as coffee or beer is a good way to bring on cramps.

To relax a cramped muscle, try a trick used by dancers to increase their flexibility. If the muscles along the back of a ballerina's legs are tight, she will tense the muscles on the front of her legs. Tensing for 20 seconds or so will relax the back of her legs. The reason: Increased tension in one group of muscles causes the opposite muscles to relax.

The same trick applies to cramps, If you have a spasm in your calf, fool it by contracting the muscles on the front of your lower leg. Stick your foot under something stationary or hold it down with the other heel and try to flex your foot. In about 20 seconds the cramps should be gone.

STAYING FLUID

Much of what we call fatigue after exercise comes from simple dehydration. Most athletes don't drink enough water. Here are some tips to keep you fluid:

- Drink before you start your workout, especially before morning workouts. You lose water as you sleep.

- By the time you feel thirsty during a workout, you are already dehydrated.

- If you plan to row for more than 40 minutes, carry a water bottle. A rule of thumb is to drink *at least* four gulps every 20 minutes during workouts. A gulp is about equal to an ounce.

- Save the juices and electrolyte solutions (like Gatorade) until after your workouts—unless they are well diluted with water. Sugar drinks tend to slosh longer in the stomach.

- Carbohydrate drinks can help performance if they are the right kind and in the right concentration. The best ones are sweetened with complex carbohydrates, "glucose polymers" or "polycose" that speed water through the stomach faster and produce less insulin rebound. Two sports drinks that satisfy these criteria are Max and Exceed.

- Before you drink anything else after a workout (like beer), drink more water.

- Very yellow urine is a sign of dehydration. Keep it clear.

PERFECTING YOUR STROKE: THE INNER QUEST

11

During the first fifty years of oarsmen in the Oxford-Cambridge Match, more than half went on to become clergymen.—BENJAMIN IVRY, *Regatta: A Celebration of Oarsmanship*

When you begin to row, the perfect stroke seems like such a readily obtainable goal. You sense that a rowing stroke has a "sweet spot" much like swinging a bat against a baseball or a racquet against a tennis ball. If you just set up for each stroke, you'll hit the sweet spot every time and a little bell of pleasure will ring in your head. The rowing stroke seems so well defined that you will eventually ring that little bell on every stroke. *Ping, ping, ping, ping.* Sooner or later, however, you'll discover that rowing isn't that way at all. The perfect stroke does not have a *ping* in the middle. The perfect stroke is one *continuous ping* that flows without a pause into yet another *ping*. Some call it *swing*. Some call it *ecstasy*. Pray for it. Pray to it. You are now on the path to madness.

Forgive me. But if you row long enough, if you let the obsession wash over you completely, you may get this way too.

When I say to you: My partner and I spent $5,000 on a new shell, took months off from our jobs to beat ourselves senseless day after day to get back into shape for the Olympic trials, and the thing that made it all worthwhile were three strokes. Three strokes! You won't nod your head and say to yourself, This guy has really lost it. You'll understand that in those three strokes time stood still, a portal to the cosmos opened up, and for an instant that stretched into eternity I felt like the most powerful sonofabitch in the universe. Too bad it happened in the semifinals.

I would not suggest that you write on your list of rowing objectives: See the face of God, but I do know that there are moments to be had in your shell when the world comes together in magical ways. I can't give you a recipe for achieving such moments, but there are some rather mundane-sounding psychological tools that may help: tools like "visualiza-

tion" and "affirmations." They are worth trying because the rewards of total commitment can be very high.

As you will probably discover, even a mental image of the perfect stroke is hard to achieve, but that image is critical if you hope to come even close to a perfect stroke on the water. If you can't visualize the perfect stroke in your head, you can't do it on the water. It's that simple. I know that now, but I had to learn it backwards.

In my first year of sweep rowing at Yale as part of the freshman "eight," I was always late: Not late to practice, but late getting my blade into the water. The other seven oar blades hit the water simultaneously and then mine dropped in a fraction of a second later. Our coach, Buzz Congram, would follow close behind our shell in his launch. During some of our practices he would call out on every single stroke. "Kiesling, you're late . . . late . . . late . . . okay . . . late. . . ." Stroke after stroke, Buzz called to me. I felt no difference when I was on time or

If you can't visualize the perfect stroke in your mind, you won't be able to create it on the water.

late. It seemed I would never be able to square my blade and drop it into the water correctly—and there was nothing at all I could do about it.

Then I noted something that surprised me about my struggle: I could not mimic that proper path of the oar blade with my hands either. Joe Bouscaren, then one of the sophomore stars on the varsity, was always pretending his arms were oars and his hands were blades. He would spread his arms out wide and take giant strokes, squaring and feathering his palms. His arms had a quick and powerful catch, just like his oars. He would squat down and even gulp air in rhythm with his strokes—as if he were racing. It was a great boost to watch him, especially since Joe had such fine technique on the water. But I couldn't get it right. It was embarrassing to think that even safely on shore waving my arms, I was late at the catch.

At that time I knew nothing about the science of using imagery to improve athletic performance. But I did notice a year or so later that once I was able to execute a good catch with my oar on the water, I could mimic it with my hands on shore—no problem. Not only that, but I could finally visualize the perfect catch in my head. I eventually discovered that if I had started by creating the right image in my mind, and had then copied the image with my hands, I could save a lot of time on the water.

Scullers like Brad Lewis and Paul Enquist have taken visualization a lot further. While they trained in the double scull for the 1984 Olympics in Los Angeles, they rehearsed each race in their heads. They imagined each race step by step, seeing themselves in the lead, feeling the fatigue, the pain, smelling the air, hearing the crowd, and watching their competitors. They went over and over these images, burning them into their brains, so that on race day, their Gold Medal performance was a matter of playing back the program.

THE ELEMENTS OF VISUALIZATION

The image must be a real possibility—something you believe is within your reach. If you are working on technique, you must be able to see what great scullers look like—either in person or from a videotape. You cannot dream up great rowing.

■ Practice the image in a quiet, meditative state. Sit or lie down in a quiet spot, close your eyes, and begin to construct the image.

■ Put flesh and bones on the image. Give it as much detail as you can—sights, sounds, smells, feelings—every sense is important.

■ Practice imagery on a regular basis— once a week is not enough. Every day for 20 minutes or so is best.

■ If possible, act out your image. Mimic the perfect stroke with your hands.

You can use imagery to help you stay motivated, to help you keep your fitness program going. Or you can use it to make yourself over. This isn't magic. We become who we think we are. We're all self-fulfilling prophecies. What imagery does is put you in the driver's seat.

THE ELEMENTS OF AFFIRMATIONS

A related but quite distinct meditative tool used by champion athletes is called affirmations. An affirmation for a sculler might be, "I hold the oar handle lightly with my fingers." If you repeat the affirmation often enough, you will in fact loosen your grip.

■ Affirmations for a sculler can be specific, such as, "I am relaxed in rough water," or, more basic, such as, "I am smooth."

■ Phrase your affirmation in a simple, direct, and *positive* way. It doesn't work to *not* do something, so formulate your affirmation in positive terms.

■ Repetition is the secret to affirmations. You must tell yourself what you want to affirm and you must tell it to yourself often.

Write down your affirmations so you'll remember when you began using them.

Practice by repeating them to yourself for a few minutes now, and work to weave them into your thoughts over the next few weeks.

ATHLETIC PROFILE

When Matthew and I began to train for the 1984 Olympic trials, we took a battery of psychological tests from a sports psychologist to determine our compatibility and predict future sources of conflict. So many elite-level athletes have taken this kind of test that there is a well-defined profile. You take the test and then worry about the parts of your profile that don't match with other athletes. Matthew and I took the test for ourselves and also for each other—filling in the answers that we thought the other would give.

The most useful lesson I learned from the test was that I am easily distracted—almost off the scale for distractibility compared to other athletes. I knew before I took the test that my mind wanders: As I row I can be daydreaming about virtually anything—at least until I crash. But until that test, I didn't realize that distractibility was a problem that I needed to work on. If I was going to steer our boat flawlessly along the 2,000-meter course, I would need to stay focused. I learned some visual focusing drill that helped me keep my mind "in the boat." One of the best was simply focusing my eyes from the tip of the cockpit to the stern of the shell. As you progress in your rowing, you may want to have this sort of evaluation done on yourself and then develop your own drills to compensate for whatever problems are found.

ROWING MEDITATION

The rhythm of the oars and the sound of water is the fastest relaxation exercise I know of. But during especially anxious times you may concentrate specifically on this rowing meditation: You'll need clear open water. Then row at an easy, regular pace. Take deep belly breaths, inhaling through your nose and exhaling through your mouth. As you exhale, concentrate on relaxing a different part of your body, starting from the feet and working up to the head. Don't worry about your state of relaxation. It will come at its own pace. You can also do this meditation on your rowing machine.

A ROWING FAMILY PORTRAIT

12

It's seven-thirty on Saturday morning at the boathouse of the New York Athletic Club in Pelham, New York, a half-hour drive from Manhattan. The sun has been up for about an hour, and it's warm and bright outside. A dredge is at work near the dock, scooping up gravel from the bottom of the channel that leads to Long Island Sound, making room for more sailboats, but no sailors are up yet: there's no wind so early in the morning. It's the perfect time for rowing and a handful of rowers are already on the dock coming in from practice. Inside one of the boat bays, someone is getting his boat down from the racks. He is about 6′2″ tall and is wearing black rowing shorts and a green T-shirt. His face is hidden at first by the 26′ long single scull balanced on the top of his head, but I can read the pink letters that ripple across the front of his shirt. MUSCLE it reads, from Madison Avenue Muscle, a body-building gym in midtown Manhattan. The shirt looks appropriate to the body. The ruddy, weathered face does not. You would expect a face twenty years younger than John McGowan's age of 52. Within moments, McGowan sets his boat gently into the water, inserts his two sculling oars into the oarlocks, climbs aboard, and pushes himself away from the dock. In a few more moments, he is almost out of sight beyond the last of the moored sailboats, rowing easily, gracefully, and fast.

John McGowan is the sales manager of Manhattan's WPIX Television and Independent Network News—a high-stress job that he balances with high-intensity exercise. The harder he works, he says, the harder he works out—and that training has made him something of a legend in the rowing community. He has won his age-group competition at this country's biggest rowing regatta, the Head of the Charles, for six years in a row—

beating former Olympians like Harvard's head coach, Harry Parker. In 1983, at the age of 47, he was fit enough to be invited to a U.S. National Team training camp, where he tested in the middle of the pack against men half his age. But one of the most remarkable things about John McGowan is that he didn't row in high school or college. He is one of a new breed of rowers. He started rowing when he was 44 in a wide, flat-bottomed sculling boat, a recreational single. Another remarkable thing about John was his partner in the 1984 Olympic trials—his son, Jim.

A few minutes after his father launches, Jim McGowan, a lanky, soft-spoken senior from Boston University, wanders into the boathouse to join a friend for a row in a double scull. Jim, a philosophy major, is taking the semester off from college to train for the 1988 Olympic trials. Says Jim, "I got into rowing about a week after my dad, when I was in ninth grade. Dad was like an alarm clock, waking me up to be on the water at five-thirty in the morning. I wanted to lie in bed. I'm not a lark, I'm more of an owl.

"Before that, Dad had been running, one of those midlife, getting-back-into-shape deals. Everything he did, he did as a workout. He does squats between points in paddle tennis. One time when I was running cross-country in high school, we ran five miles together. I was running easily, just a step ahead of him, feeling terrific, and he was really straining to keep up. And then when we got home, he unzipped his jacket and underneath he was wearing a 30-pound weight vest.

"The first time I beat my dad in practice was the summer after my freshman year in college. Losing was no big deal to

him, but winning meant a lot to me." When the two men first rowed together in a double scull, Jim was a lot smaller than his father and his oarlocks were adjusted to make his load lighter. Now 6'5" and 195 pounds, Jim is the strongest rower in the family. "When I'm home I practice with my dad," says Jim. "For short distances he's as fast as anybody at the club, though his recovery time is a lot longer—or at least he thinks it is. When my partner [for the 1988 Olympic trials] hurt his back, I was going to ask my dad to row with me. Sometimes rowing has nothing to do with fitness. We mesh well together."

A few minutes after Jim and his partner paddled away from the dock, his mother, Carol McGowan, arrived at the boathouse. She's a warm, energetic woman—who lets on that she has to be athletic to keep up with her family. This morning she is in a hurry because she has a tennis match following her row, and a golf game scheduled after that. Says Carol, "I had to learn to row if I was going to see my family. At first everyone was worried about me. There were a lot of myths around back then—that a woman my age would never be strong enough to row, or that it would be bad for my health. Everybody was very protective of me." There were other difficulties as well. "When you start waking up at five-fifteen in the morning, you begin to wonder if this is a serious problem. I was scared at first. I don't like swimming. They held the stern of my boat against the dock while I practiced. Then I started to love it, the sunrises especially."

Carol rowed her first race in a double scull with her husband. In her first race alone in a single scull, oddly enough, her husband was declared the winner. He was coaching her from his own single

John, Carol, and Jim McGowan after practice at the New York Athletic Club in Pelham.

Both John and Carol started out in Aldens. After a few months John was rowing faster than many of the local rowers in racing singles, so he decided it was time to move up.

and crossed the finish line first. Now that Carol is 50, she has moved into a new age category for the Head of the Charles. She's confident that she can win because she rows very well, and because there are not yet that many women her age who compete.

The McGowans' two daughters both learned to row at a family vacation at the Craftsbury Sculling School in Vermont, but they don't get out on the water as often as they used to. Alison, 18, won a handful of junior rowing medals in high school, but is more interested in horse-back riding. Karen, 24, does not row so much because, in her brother's words, "she gets too much encouragement to row from the family."

John McGowan was a competitive swimmer in his youth, but says he gave it up before he had a chance to really find out how good he was. At age 30 he started jogging to get back in shape. He wasn't a very fast runner naturally, so he started adding weight to increase the challenge and the strain. Eventually he

The McGowans are actually a three-ergometer family, but Jim had taken one of the ergs to college.

was running his four-mile loop wearing two 30-pound weight vests and 20 more pounds worth of ankle and hand weights hidden underneath his warmup suit. "He looked like the Michelin tire man," jokes Carol. "The neighbors asked me if he had lost his mind."

John McGowan spent his first year and a half rowing in a recreational single, at first plugging away behind the more experienced men in their racing shells, and then plugging away in front of them. He says there is no secret to how he got so fast: He trained harder than anyone else. In 1984 he was doing the same thirteen workouts each week as the U.S. Olympic squad, while working full time. He managed by keeping most of his paper work in computer diskettes that could be easily transported from the computer in his office to his computer at home. For workouts, he rowed at the N.Y.A.C. club or on one of the McGowans' three Concept II rowing ergometers. When John was training for the 1984 Olympic trials, he would ship an ergometer with him on business trips.

All that training was a strain on their marriage. They didn't get invited out much, and when they did, John would announce that he had to leave at nine o'clock. Not all their friends understood. On the other hand, says Carol, "If you have a gift for something, holding back isn't good for you." John has since cut back on his training to what he considers a maintenance level, and he no longer travels with an ergometer—he calls the company that makes the machines to find local health clubs that have them wherever he goes. And rowing may have other drawbacks as well. After her brief row, Carol McGowan rushed off to her tennis game. An hour and a half later, when her court time was up, she felt like she was still warming up.

GETTING SERIOUS   13

I remember returning a few days later to the ergometer room that had been set up at the Dartmouth Medical School. There were about forty oarsmen still in contention for the U.S. Team, few enough that they could start to scan our insides. My legs ached as I walked through corridors filled with lab-coated medical technicians, and for a moment I was brought back to the familiar trudge into my freshman biology lab; this time, however, I was the white rat.

As in the previous ergometer piece, cardiac monitors were taped to my chest with wires running out under my shirt. My hand was then placed in a bowl of warm water to dilate the capillaries. Simultaneously with pricking my finger, they stabbed the inside of my elbow. Measuring lactates in my blood, they told me, but I was so nervous that my blood refused to flow. Later they would try multiple lacerations of my earlobe.

Once on the ergometer, I was connected to a gas exchange monitor. They plugged my nose and inserted a snorkel in my mouth that was connected by flexible tubing to a computer that spewed ticker tape. The mouthpiece was supported by a clear plastic frame connected to a headband. A valve in the snorkel allowed me to breathe outside air but exhale only into the machine, which would then measure the amount of oxygen I used and the carbon dioxide I produced as I rowed to exhaustion. These measurements gave an indication of how much work I was capable of. . . . What surprised me was the disparity between the aerobic and anaerobic capacities of different world-class oarsmen. All that proves was they had superior strength, better technique, or a higher tolerance for pain.

STEPHEN KIESLING, The Shell Game

That was in 1979 at the U.S. National Team Selection Camp, when sophisticated sports testing seemed like a reward for world-class athletes, and, so far as I could tell, before anybody really knew what to do with the data that was collected. It was a wonderful time for sports medicine: all potential and no apparent limits. The nation had discovered running and was pushing toward the first triathlon. Overenthusiastic physicians proclaimed that if you could run a marathon, you would never suffer a heart attack. Peak performance and optimum health were widely regarded as the same thing.

Not long after that, of course, several very fit and visible people dropped dead—including Jack Kelly, head of the U.S. Olympic Committee and a former Olympic Gold medalist in the single scull. These days, sales of walking shoes are surpassing sales of running shoes and even Olympic athletes feel mortal. If you want to live forever, your best bet is probably to walk every day. On the other hand, rowing—and becoming very fit—is a lot more fun.

Andy Messer, a Canadian Olympian, on an old-style Gammut ergometer at Yale. Note the hand of the coxswain, who writes down split times and stroke ratings to keep the rower honest.

YOUR PERSONAL PERFORMANCE LAB

Thanks to all the years of research, it is now fairly easy to design a personalized rowing program that will quickly get you in very good shape. Before you set up your program, however, you should understand some of the basics of fitness.

Working out is a cycle of stress and rebuilding. It begins with a healthy dose of exercise stress. Then the stressed systems have to rebuild. When the renovation is complete, usually 24 to 48 hours later, the body is just a little bit stronger, more efficient, and fitter. It's ready then for another cycle of exercise and recovery. The secret to getting the most out of these cycles is in knowing just how much stress to apply, how to apply it, and how long to allow for recovery. In other words, the three critical factors that you need to consider when you set up your program are:

Intensity   How hard you should work out

Duration   How long you should work out

Frequency   How often you should work out

Most often people focus on just one of the three factors without considering the other components. As you will discover, there are good reasons for juggling all three factors from one workout to the next.

The Energy Continuum: Easy Paddling to 100% and Beyond

To get a better sense of how different intensities affect your training, join me on a progressive workout from paddling to flat-out sprinting on my rowing ergometer.

Paddling—the fat burner: I'm paddling easily and my heart rate is about 110 beats per minute—about the same as if I were walking briskly. As I paddle, my working muscles are fueled primarily by fat stored throughout my body. I'm breathing easily. My heart is pumping blood at less than full volume on each stroke. All these things help explain why easy paddling is a great beginning exercise— especially for people who are overweight. It burns fat directly without putting a lot of strain on the heart.

60%—the base of aerobics, endurance and recovery pace: I'm breathing a little faster, my heart rate is now 120 beats per minute, and the volume of blood pumped by each beat has reached its maximum. This is the "aerobic threshold," the point at which I have put enough strain on my circulatory system so that I will begin to improve my fitness. It's called aerobic because the muscles use an energy system that requires oxygen. The fuel I'm burning is mainly glycogen rather than fat. Glycogen is a much better fuel: The only problem is, I have a lot bigger store of fat than glycogen.

Most research indicates that exercising below this threshold probably won't improve your fitness significantly. If you stay just above this threshold you will improve your body's ability to transport oxygen. Long and low-intensity workouts stimulate the growth of capillaries that bring more oxygen to the working muscles.

70%—the training zone: My heart rate continues to climb steadily. My muscles are using fuel so quickly now that my aerobic system is not completely able to keep up with the demand. Gradually my muscles are shifting to an energy system that does not require oxygen—the anaerobic system. Many people think that there is a sudden shift from the aerobic to anaerobic system, but all exercise has both aerobic and anaerobic components. The more intense the exercise, the more anaerobic it becomes.

The anaerobic system produces the waste product lactic acid or lactate, which is dumped out of the muscles into the bloodstream. I don't feel the acid yet, but the slight increase in the acidity of my blood is a signal to my lungs to breathe faster. Exhaling carbon dioxide reduces the amount of acid in the blood.

My breathing rate has increased—but it's still steady. If I were running at this pace, a full cycle of inhaling and exhaling would take me four foot strikes. Steady breathing is a good indication that I can maintain this pace for a long time. A good test for this kind of pace is the Talk Test. At this healthy pace I can just carry on a conversation.

80%—anaerobic threshold (AT): *Doctor's okay required.* My next step is the anaerobic threshold, which for most people corresponds to somewhere between 150 and 180 heartbeats per minute. Probably a better term than anaerobic threshold is OBLA (Onset of Blood Lactate Accumulation). What happens is that lactic acid is dumped out of the muscles much faster than it can be removed from the bloodstream. When lactate accumulates the blood becomes more acidic. I am beginning to feel a burning sensation in my thigh muscles.

In most sports, when you reach this threshold, your breathing rate increases dramatically to blow off the extra carbon dioxide. If I were running I might suddenly switch from inhaling every fourth step to every second step. When you're rowing it's harder to note the change in breathing rhythm so precisely because it's linked or *entrained* to your stroke rate. At this pace, I can no longer carry on a conversation.

If I were just interested in being in great shape and not planning to compete, I would never need to push to this level, or at least not beyond it. You can become very fit by training just below the breathing shift. If you are just starting a competitive training program, you should spend your first couple of months rowing below this intensity to build what's known as an aerobic base. Your body needs that time to develop the blood supply to the muscles.

90%—long-interval race training: Interval training is where the mind games get serious. Do I really care about the race coming up? Maybe I've been pushing too hard recently. Maybe no one will notice if I slack off now. . . . After a few minutes this pace can be really uncomfortable and the amount of time you can sustain your workout drops.

100%—maximum aerobic capacity (VO2 max): Heart rate 190 beats per minute. This is still not the absolute limit of performance—I can still push harder—but it's the limit of my heart, lungs, and peripheral circulatory system to deliver oxygen as fuel. When you reach your VO2 max, your heart rate has peaked. It can't beat any faster. If you have been rowing regularly, you should be able to maintain this pace for about 8 minutes *when you really want to.*

Beyond 100%—short intervals: If you have a high tolerance for lactic acid and for pain, you may be able to go a lot harder than 100% for a short time—usually less than 1 minute.

Cool Down: A Part of Every Workout

In a shell, you almost always have to cool down after a hard workout because you have to row back to shore and then carry your boat in. One of the potential dangers of working out on a rowing machine, however, is that you can push your body to 100% or beyond, and then stop cold. For example, the phone rings and you leap up to get it. You then feel dizzy, lightheaded, even nauseated. What happens when you abruptly stop exercising is that your heart rate and blood pressure plummet. Blood pools in your legs and makes you dizzy. Almost immediately, your body responds to the drop with a surge of adrenalin to bring your blood pressure back up. That sort of jolt could kill you.

I always finish my machine or shell workouts with at least 5 minutes of firm paddling or half-pressure rowing to cool down after a strenuous workout. The cool-down period allows the pulse to drop gradually and the muscles to flush out the various waste products. East German rowers cool down for 20 minutes or more after races.

For the next hour stay warm: During the first hour or so after a strenuous workout, your immune system is weak and you are more susceptible to disease. So cover up with sweat clothes. Some international teams quarantine their athletes for an hour or so after each race to help prevent them from becoming ill.

THE CONTINUUM IN PERSPECTIVE

If you are looking for health, you need never push harder than 60 to 80%. Once you push at 80% or more, you have crossed the threshold from healthy exercise to athletic training. The good news is that you can raise your VO2 max and your absolute maximum without ever pushing any higher than 80%. A long race, like the Head of the Charles (3½ miles or 5,700 meters), is an 80% race. The fastest crews race at their anaerobic threshold but no higher—at least not for more than a few strokes. Endurance events that take several hours—like the 34-mile Round Manhattan Race or the 32-nautical mile Catalina Race—are even lower intensity, closer to 70%.

If you want to race at an elite level in a standard 2,000-meter event, however, you'll have to sustain 95–100% or more for all 7 minutes. All things considered, the Head of the Charles is a more pleasant race to prepare for and compete in than a 2,000-meter event.

YOUR PERSONAL PROGRAM

14

> Much of what we call aging is not getting worn out but lack of use. . . . We assume that effort causes the fatigue that wears us down. In fact, we become fatigued because we don't do enough.—JOHN JEROME, author, masters swimmer, and ergometer rower

The goal of this chapter is to establish a program of specific workouts to match your current level of fitness. If you are new to sports, this may be a major turning point. It is a chance to put sports science on your side and to gain a lot more from the time and effort you spend in your boat. You can enjoy the best shape of your life. On the other hand, if you start worrying about training before you are comfortable in your boat or on your ergometer, you may just take the joy out of your rowing. Take your time. Ideally you should have been rowing at least three times a week for 6 to 8 weeks. You should be able to row continuously for 20 or 30 minutes—and be able to push yourself up to full pressure with confidence for several minutes.

You learned in Chapter 13 that as you pull harder on your oars, as you go from paddling to quarter pressure to half pressure and up to a full sprint, your body passes through phases. You start out breathing easily, then faster, then you are panting, and, finally, you're out of breath. These stages are separated by thresholds along what is called the energy continuum. In order to create a scientific training program, you need to understand your own energy continuum. You need to know *your* thresholds: what they are and where they are. It's pretty easy if you take it a step at a time.

Your first step toward building a personalized training program is to take a test to establish your VO2 max (Maximum Oxygen Uptake) on the energy continuum. From that test you will be able to calculate the intensity and duration of four basic fitness workouts and two advanced competition workouts.

Take the test on a Concept II ergometer rather than in a shell. As you row on the machine, pay attention to how you feel as you push yourself—your PE (Perceived Exertion). You should also try out each of the workouts on an ergometer to see how they feel—to calibrate your PE so that you can match that effort in your shell.

Basic Workouts

1. **Endurance workouts:** 60% intensity. Your longest workout to be done once a week when you have plenty of time.
2. **Standard workouts:** 70% intensity. Your bread-and-butter fitness workout at least once a week.
3. **Recovery workouts:** 60% intensity. Light, relaxing skill-and-drill workouts for promoting recovery. Light exercise is often better than complete rest.
4. **Anaerobic threshold workouts:** 80% intensity. Your fourth or fifth weekly workout—the edge of competitive training. Before you add one of these, you should be doing at least one of each of the first three.

Competition Workouts

5. **Long-interval workouts:** 90–100% for 3 to 7 minutes. Training for competition.
6. **Short-interval workouts:** Flat out for about 1 minute. Preparing to peak for a race.

Don't let these percentages intimidate you. From the test, you will begin to develop a very accurate sense of how hard you are rowing. You'll know the difference between 60 and 70%, and you'll be able to do it again and again.

THE ENTRANCE EXAM—100%

The test is to row a 2,500-meter piece on a Concept II ergometer, a newer machine with the computer Performance Monitor, not the old-style odometer. If you don't have access to a Concept II, call the company to find a local health club that has one. You can almost always get a free one-time visitor's pass from a health club, although you may have to sit through a membership sales pitch. If possible, do a couple of workouts on the machine before you take the test so that you will be familiar with how it feels. Take this test on a day when you are well rested and energetic—not the day after a hard workout or after you've been up all night. It may help to have a friend along to offer encouragement and to monitor your stroke rate.

Pulse vs. Perceived Exertion

If you have access to an accurate pulse monitor, wear it during the test to help calibrate your perceived exertion with your actual heart rate. Unfortunately, the only worthwhile pulse monitors are the expensive kind (about $250) that have a chest-strap sensor connected to a wristwatch display. Fingertip monitors, earlobe monitors, and wristwatch monitors are unreliable. If you have to buy a pulse monitor, however, it is probably not worth the money. Most recent evidence shows that PE works very well. It also takes into account factors such as fatigue, level of fitness, heat, altitude, the type of exercise, and in *some* cases even the effects of some drugs that affect heart rate. Those adjustments are generally often ignored by pulse counters.

Ergometer Settings

Set the chain on the large chain ring
Close the air vents on the side of the fan
Set the computer to Pace/Meters (split time per 500 meters)

Pre-test Warmup

3 minutes of paddling
3 minutes of three-quarter pressure
Three 10-stroke pieces, full pressure
One or more 20-stroke pieces

The Test

Set the monitor to count down from 2,500 meters to zero.

Row! Try to maintain a hard, even pace at the highest stroke rating that you can sustain in your shell.

Immediately after you finish, count your pulse for 15 seconds and multiply by four to calculate your pulse rate per minute.

The key to the test is to establish a steady pace that you can sustain for the duration (7–14 minutes). Your goal is to finish with no energy left, as if you had rowed a hard, close race. Pay attention to how you feel as you row so you will be able to match it when you move from the ergometer to your shell.

When you have completed your 2,500 meters, record your time. You will use it to calculate the intensity and duration of your future workouts using the training tables in this chapter. You should also keep track of your stroke cadence.

To see how you rank in the world of rowing, compare your time to rowers of your own age all over the world in the Concept II Ergometer World Rankings on page 124. If your first results are not very encouraging, don't worry about it. The next time you attempt this test, after three weeks or so, you will probably improve dramatically.

YOUR INTENSITY PROFILE

Now that you know your time for 2,500 meters, you can use the chart to create your own exercise Intensity Profile. Find your Total Time on the far-left column of the Pace Training Table. Your 100% Max-Pace (your average 500-meter split time) is in the second column. To the right are the four different paces from 60 to 90% that you'll use in your workouts. Draw a line on the chart to mark your paces. Write the date beside it.

YOUR DURATION PROFILE

Next, use your time for the 2,500 meters to calculate your Duration Profile, the six different durations you will use in your workouts. Find your Total Time in the left-hand column of the Workout Durations table and draw a line under that row of durations.

Ergometer Durations: The duration profile is calibrated for on-the-water workouts. Machine workouts lack some of the thrills of water, but they do concentrate time wonderfully. For the four "basic workouts," your durations on an erg will generally be about ⅔ as long as the times listed on the table. Experiment. My *longest* ergo workouts tend to be only 45 minutes to an hour—half my longest water workouts.

INTENSITY PROFILE

CONCEPT II PACE TRAINING TABLES—PACES

2,500 m Test Results		Training Paces (min:sec per 500 m)			
Total Time	MaxPace	60% pace	70% pace	80% pace	90% pace
13:50	2:46	3:18	3:08	3:00	2:52
13:40	2:44	3:16	3:06	2:58	2:50
13:30	2:42	3:14	3:04	2:56	2:48
13:25	2:41	3:12	3:02	2:54	2:47
13:15	2:39	3:10	3:00	2:52	2:45
13:05	2:37	3:07	2:58	2:50	2:43
12:55	2:35	3:05	2:56	2:48	2:41
12:45	2:33	3:03	2:53	2:46	2:39
12:35	2:31	3:01	2:51	2:44	2:37
12:25	2:29	2:59	2:49	2:42	2:35
12:20	2:28	2:56	2:47	2:40	2:33
12:10	2:26	2:54	2:45	2:38	2:31
12:00	2:24	2:52	2:43	2:36	2:29
11:50	2:22	2:50	2:41	2:34	2:27
11:40	2:20	2:48	2:39	2:32	2:25
11:30	2:18	2:45	2:37	2:30	2:24
11:25	2:17	2:43	2:35	2:28	2:22
11:15	2:15	2:41	2:32	2:26	2:20
11:05	2:13	2:39	2:30	2:24	2:18
10:55	2:11	2:36	2:28	2:22	2:16
10:45	2:09	2:34	2:26	2:20	2:14
10:35	2:07	2:32	2:24	2:18	2:12
10:25	2:05	2:30	2:22	2:16	2:10
10:20	2:04	2:28	2:20	2:14	2:08
10:10	2:02	2:25	2:18	2:12	2:06
10:00	2:00	2:23	2:16	2:10	2:04
9:50	1:58	2:21	2:14	2:08	2:02
9:40	1:56	2:19	2:12	2:06	2:00
9:30	1:54	2:17	2:09	2:04	1:59
9:20	1:52	2:14	2:07	2:02	1:57
9:15	1:51	2:12	2:05	2:00	1:55
9:05	1:49	2:10	2:03	1:58	1:53
8:55	1:47	2:08	2:01	1:56	1:51
8:45	1:45	2:06	1:59	1:54	1:49
8:35	1:43	2:03	1:57	1:52	1:47
8:25	1:41	2:01	1:55	1:50	1:45
8:15	1:39	1:59	1:53	1:48	1:43
8:10	1:38	1:57	1:51	1:46	1:41
8:00	1:36	1:54	1:48	1:44	1:39
7:50	1:34	1:52	1:46	1:42	1:37
7:40	1:32	1:50	1:44	1:40	1:36
7:30	1:30	1:48	1:42	1:38	1:34
7:20	1:28	1:46	1:40	1:36	1:32
7:15	1:27	1:43	1:38	1:34	1:30

Stroke Rate:

DURATION PROFILE

TRAINING TABLES—WORKOUT DURATIONS

2,500 m Test Results		Training Durations (hrs:min:sec)					
		Intervals		Other Workouts		Anaerobic	
Total Time	MaxPace	Short	Long	Recovery	Std.	Threshold	Endurance
13:50	2:46	1:00	5:00	0:15:00	0:15:00	0:24:00	0:45:00
13:40	2:44	1:00	5:00	0:15:00	0:15:00	0:24:00	0:45:00
13:30	2:42	1:00	5:00	0:15:00	0:15:00	0:24:00	0:45:00
13:25	2:41	1:00	5:00	0:15:00	0:15:00	0:24:00	0:45:00
13:15	2:39	1:00	5:00	0:15:00	0:15:00	0:24:00	0:45:00
13.05	2:37	1:00	5:00	0:15:00	0:15:00	0:24:00	0:45:00
12:55	2:35	1:00	5:00	0:15:00	0:15:00	0:24:00	0:45:00
12:45	2:33	1:00	5:00	0:15:00	0:15:00	0:24:00	0:45:00
12:35	2:31	1:00	5:00	0:15:00	0:15:00	0:24:00	0:45:00
12:25	2:29	1:00	5:00	0:15:00	0:15:00	0:24:00	0:45:00
12:20	2:28	1:00	5:00	0:15:00	0:15:00	0:24:00	0:45:00
12:10	2:26	1:00	5:00	0:15:00	0:15:00	0:24:00	0:45:00
12:00	2:24	1:00	5:00	0:15:00	0:15:00	0:24:00	0:45:00
11:50	2:22	1:00	5:00	0:15:00	0:15:00	0:24:00	0:45:00
11:40	2:20	1:00	5:00	0:20:00	0:20:00	0:30:00	1:00:00
11:30	2:20	1:00	5:00	0:20:00	0:20:00	0:30:00	1:00:00
11:25	2:17	1:00	5:00	0:20:00	0:20:00	0:30:00	1:00:00
11:15	2:15	1:00	5:00	0:20:00	0:20:00	0:30:00	1:00:00
11:05	2:13	1:00	5:00	0:20:00	0:20:00	0:30:00	1:00:00
10:55	2:11	1:00	5:00	0:20:00	0:20:00	0:30:00	1:00:00
10:45	2:09	1:00	5:00	0:20:00	0:20:00	0:30:00	1:00:00
10:35	2:07	1:00	5:00	0:20:00	0:20:00	0:30:00	1:00:00
10:25	2:05	1:00	5:00	0:20:00	0:20:00	0:30:00	1:00:00
10:20	2:04	1:00	5:00	0:20:00	0:20:00	0:30:00	1:00:00
10:10	2:02	1:00	5:00	0:20:00	0:20:00	0:30:00	1:00:00
10:00	2:00	1:00	5:00	0:20:00	0:20:00	0:30:00	1:00:00
9:50	1:58	1:00	5:00	0:30:00	0:30:00	0:45:00	1:30:00
9:40	1:56	1:00	5:00	0:30:00	0:30:00	0:45:00	1:30:00
9:30	1:54	1:00	5:00	0:30:00	0:30:00	0:45:00	1:30:00
9:20	1:52	1:00	5:00	0:30:00	0:30:00	0:45:00	1:30:00
9:15	1:51	1:00	5:00	0:30:00	0:30:00	0:45:00	1:30:00
9:05	1:49	1:00	5:00	0:30:00	0:45:00	1:00:00	2:00:00
8:55	1:47	1:00	5:00	0:30:00	0:45:00	1:00:00	2:00:00
8:45	1:45	1:00	5:00	0:30:00	0:45:00	1:00:00	2:00:00
8:35	1:43	1:00	5:00	0:30:00	0:45:00	1:00:00	2:00:00
8:25	1:41	1:00	5:00	0:30:00	0:45:00	1:00:00	2:00:00
8:15	1:39	1:00	5:00	0:30:00	0:45:00	1:00:00	2:00:00
8:10	1:38	1:00	5:00	0:30:00	0:45:00	1:00:00	2:00:00
8:00	1:36	1:00	5:00	0:30:00	0:45:00	1:00:00	2:00:00
7:50	1:34	1:00	5:00	0:30:00	0:45:00	1:00:00	2:00:00
7:40	1:32	1:00	5:00	0:30:00	0:45:00	1:00:00	2:00:00
7:30	1:30	1:00	5:00	0:30:00	0:45:00	1:00:00	2:00:00
7:20	1:28	1:00	5:00	0:30:00	0:45:00	1:00:00	2:00:00
7:15	1:27	1:00	5:00	0:30:00	0:45:00	1:00:00	2:00:00

YOUR FREQUENCY PROFILE

Your optimum frequency—how often you should exercise—can be a delicate balance. If you exercise too often, you don't allow your body time to recover, and you may become sick or injured. If you don't exercise often enough, you won't improve. To be safe, change your frequency gradually. If you have been rowing only two or three times a week, it is a bad idea to suddenly switch to five or six times a week. You'll quickly feel stale and find reasons to quit.

To determine your Frequency Profile use your workout logbook or your memory to reconstruct your last month of exercise on the following calendar. Just put a mark for every day you worked out. Be honest with yourself. If you have not been exercising much, your profile will be mostly blank.

PUTTING IT ALL TOGETHER

	M	T	W	T	F	S	S
WK1							
WK2							
WK3							
WK4							

How many times a week on average do you exercise? _____

Now that you know the workouts, there are only a few more rules of thumb to consider as you set your schedule:

1. To maintain or gain fitness, you have to exercise at least three times a week. If you leave more than three days between workout sessions, your gains will be canceled out. In effect, your body will adapt to its nonexercising rather than its exercising state.

2. It takes about 48 hours for the body to repair the damage created by a hard workout and to completely replenish fuel supplies. The most you should do the day after a stressful workout is a recovery workout.

3. Never increase your total exercise by more than 10% a week. Increases of 10 to 15% every three weeks make more sense. Tendons, ligaments, and muscles have to be reshaped; bone has to be rebuilt; enzymatic and physiological systems have to be tuned up to work at higher levels—all this takes time.

4. Three weeks is about how long it takes your body to plateau at a given level of exercise stress. After three weeks at the same level of effort you will stop improving—until you increase your weekly exercise.

	BEGINNER	INTERMEDIATE	ADVANCED
MON.	Off	Recovery	Recovery
TUES.	Recovery	Standard	Standard
WED.	Off	Off	Recovery
THUR.	Standard	Speed	Speed
FRI.	Off	Off	Recovery
SAT.	Endurance	Recovery	A.T.
SUN.	Off	Endurance	Endurance

Making Waves

The final thing to consider as you schedule your workouts is to make waves. The best training programs create waves of increasing workout stress—usually increased over several days—followed by wave troughs—recovery periods—followed by another wave, and so on. Many training programs have waves upon waves built into them.

For a beginning rower, when you put the three workouts together on your weekly schedule, you would do your endurance workout first, say, on Saturday morning. Follow it by a recovery workout on Tuesday, and finish the week with a standard workout on Thursday. This creates a wave of varying intensity. The peak of the wave is your endurance workout. It's followed by a wave trough with the recovery workout. Then you start building a new wave after that with your standard workouts, building toward your next endurance workouts. These three workouts may seem like a light load, even to begin with, but it's the best way to start. The really important thing is to establish this first wave of training and then build on it.

If you're already exercising three times a week and are ready for more, you can create two or three waves per week. Once again, you start from the top of the list, with an endurance workout, a standard workout, and a recovery workout, but then both an anaerobic threshold workout and another recovery—for a total of five workouts per week.

Once again, look to establish a wave of training. Start out with a peak on Sunday with your endurance workout. On Monday you drop to a recovery workout, and Tuesday you start building again with a standard workout—building toward another crest on Thursday with an anaerobic threshold workout. You would take Friday off and then beginning a slight rise with a recovery workout on Saturday and another peak on Sunday.

Advanced Workouts

No matter what level athlete you are or you become, those four basic workouts will remain an essential part of your repertoire. But for competition, you'll need to expand that list to include interval workouts. These advanced workouts are very strenuous and potentially dangerous. If you have any doubts about your health, check with a doctor before you try them. And the ability to complete them does not necessarily mean that you are a healthier person for doing them. These workouts are about performance, *not* health.

Interval workouts consist of hard high-intensity spurts alternating with low-intensity rest intervals. The *interval* in workouts actually refers to the rest time and the secret to making these workouts effective is in managing that rest period. Interval workouts boost anaerobic power and strength, but most of all to raise your maximum oxygen consumption to its peak. There are two main types of intervals—long and short. Both hurt.

Long intervals mean pushing yourself at your 100% pace for about 5 minutes and then slowing down to your endurance intensity until you feel just able to do it again—usually about 3 to 4 minutes. These long intervals would be preceded by a long warmup and repeated 3 to 6 times—however many you can complete and still maintain your intensity. Finish your workout with a long cool-down.

Short intervals may be even tougher. After a long warmup, sprint flat-out for 60 to 90 seconds, paddle for another 60 to 90 seconds, and sprint again. Do from 6 to 15 intervals. Some athletes and coaches use even shorter, more frequent, repetitions, but the higher speeds involved in these workouts make them too dangerous. You should attempt them only under the direction of an experienced coach.

Program Design Worksheet

	M	T	W	T	F	S	S
WK1							
WK2							
WK3							
WK4							
WK5							
WK6							
WK7							
WK8							
WK9							
WK10							
WK11							
WK12							
TOTAL							

Interval Waves

Both these workouts can be incorporated into waves: Interval workouts can create an interval wave—a recovery workout followed by an interval workout. Interval waves most *always* be followed by a recovery workout or a day off. Serious competitors trying to peak for a competition may have their entire week made up of two interval waves and an endurance wave. Anaerobic threshold workouts can help in the early stages of a peaking cycle, but they may not be necessary if you're competing regularly. Interval workouts can help bring you to a peak, but they are hard to keep up for more than twelve to fifteen weeks. Save them for the last few months leading up to an important competition. Once the competition season begins, make sure you factor your races into your workout program just like any other high-intensity workout. If you're competing regularly, you don't need as many hard workouts.

Now use what you've learned to pencil in your own twelve-week workout program.

BUILDING A LOGBOOK

As every athlete knows, the best coaches set their workout schedules well in advance and then fine-tune individual workouts or change them completely, depending on how each athlete performs. The secret to coaching yourself is much the same: Write down your own workout schedule in advance and then carefully keep track of how your body responds to the program you set up. You'll not only have the satisfaction of quantifying your improvements, you'll see patterns in your life that weren't evident before. You'll sense progress and be able to push for peaks. Maybe more importantly, you'll get an early warning of oncoming illness or injury so you can change your schedule before you fall too far.

REMEMBER: Detail is something you can't get enough of when you are looking back and trying to figure out what went right or wrong.

Record your daily workouts: Write down the intensity, duration, and time of your workouts. This information will provide a picture of the rhythm of your training and reveal patterns that may have contributed to your ups and downs.

Monitor three stress indicators: Exercise gives extra energy, but working too hard can bring both champion athletes and beginners to their knees. They fall into a long period of feeling tired and low on energy that leaves them susceptible to

flus and colds. Surprisingly, aspiring novices actually overtrain as often as Olympic athletes because they also try to do too much too soon. Three signs that the overtraining monster may be stalking you come from your weight, resting pulse, and sleep patterns.

Body weight: Weigh yourself on rising every morning or at some other set time of day. What matters is the trend in your weight and how much your weight on a given day might fall below that trend. A rapid drop in weight is a signal you are overdoing it. The best way to keep track is to calculate your average weight each week. If your weight falls more than 4 pounds in a day or two, that is an indication that you may be overtraining. If you are a small person, weighing around 100 pounds, use 3 pounds as your indicator. If you are near or over 200 pounds, use 5 pounds.

Morning pulse: Before you get out of bed each morning take your pulse. A 6-beat-per-minute or greater increase in your resting heart rate is a sign that your body is working overtime to recover from too much stress or is fighting illness.

Sleep patterns: Keep track of when you go to sleep and when you wake up. As a rule, any unplanned change of more than half an hour in your sleep pattern—if you couldn't sleep soundly or if you couldn't wake up easily—is worth watching. The need for extra sleep can be an indication that your body is working hard at recovering. Not being able to sleep is often a sign of too much stress. Some scientists feel that *when* you get your hours of sleep is just as important as *how* much sleep you get. Going to sleep as little as 40 minutes later than normal coupled with less sleep overall can be a bad combination.

No single stress indicators should stop you from training. But if two or three of these caution lights are flashing, you should probably take it easy until things get back to normal.

Learn from your log: On a quiet day when you have a little time on your hands, take a few moments to go back over your logs. Look for patterns. When you felt best, what preceded that moment? When you felt worst, is there anything to indicate why?

The Concept II Ergometer World Ranking

	Women		Men	
5–19	K. Stoddard	9:06.03	P. Sharis	7:37.3
	10%	9:55		8:24
	50%	10:51		9:07
20–29	A. Fuller	8:30.4	M. Siekkowski	7:15.5
	10%	9:23		8:02
	50%	10:22		8:44
30–39	A. Peck	8:56.3	J. Biglow	7:40.3
	10%	10:03		8:30
	50%	11:16		9:21
40–49	V. Scott	9:23.0	K. Foote	7:50.9
	10%	10:12		8:38
	50%	11:45		9:2
50–59	L. Daly	9:53.3	A. Laundon	8:08.3
	10%	10:58		8:43
	50%	12:17		9:00
60–69	D. Everett	11:26.4	H. Everett	8:25.0
	10%	11:34		9:09
	50%	13:20		11:04
70–79	B. Bunce	12:54	J. Clinard	10:09
	10%	12:54		10:54
	50%	13:45		10:54
80–89			C. Coumes	12:33
			50%	12:50

Above is a summary of the more than 5,800 entries in the 1989 Concept II World Ranking gathered from fourteen countries. I have included the record time, the top 10%, and the top 50% to give you an idea of the range. When you are happy with your own score, send it in. If you have a record breaker, it must be submitted from an organized public or club race.

RACING

15

Ratings from a champion: "The ideal stroke rating for a 2,000 meter race is about 32 or 33 strokes per minute. During the final sprint, my rating goes up to 35 or 36. At the Head of the Charles, I try to row at 31 the entire way." JOE BOUSCAREN, M.D.

NOTE: When you're starting out, your stroke rating may be closer to 20 strokes per minute. Perfect your technique before you raise your rating.

In my freshman year of rowing, I viewed the spring racing season as the price we had to pay for the thrills and camaraderie of training through the fall and winter. I was not eager to put that training to the test. The ritual that was supposed to ready us for each Saturday's race served most of all to fill me with dread. Practices on Mondays and Tuesdays were still glorious—just hard rowing for 4- or 5-minute pieces. Wednesday was another hard practice—five or six 2- or 3-minute pieces rowed at or above our racing cadence. But any exhilaration was overshadowed by the knowledge that it was the last real work before the race. On Thursday, the "taper" would begin: We would do a warmup, practice our "starts," and then do two or three 500-meter pieces. If the pieces went well, we told each other that the race would go well. If the pieces went badly, we told each other that we had gotten the bad rowing out of our systems—that the race would still go well. On Friday afternoon we would ride the bus to the race site and row over the course to learn the landmarks. We almost always raced the same distance, 2,000 meters, but each new course seemed infinitely longer than that. We would then go to dinner and wolf down enough pasta to fuel us through a marathon or two. Feeling both nervous and bloated, we would go back to our hotel rooms and try to sleep. During the long warmup before the race, I would invariably feel exhausted—much too tired to complete the distance. At the starting line of the Eastern Championships, one of my teammates summed up my feelings for all those early races: He threw up.

But no memories from those first years of rowing are nearly so vivid as those minutes when another crew was beside us, when the dread dissolved and we rowed our hearts out, or maybe we

When you race, you may surprise yourself.

didn't. Each race lasted somewhere between 6 and 7 minutes, but they seemed to go on for as many seconds or as many hours. Races were so frightening because they were supposed to encapsulate a whole year of experience—yet, ultimately, they were so wonderful because they did.

Nowadays I can think of few things more joyful than rowing a race. Fortunately, there are a growing number of events that enable rowers of any age and skill to experience the thrill of racing. The competition can seem quite serious on the starting line, but there is a real sense of striving together to bring out the best in everyone. When competitors say good luck, they mean it. Essentially, each race is an excuse for a picnic and a party among old and new friends.

There are different kinds of races: 2,000-meter sprints, head races, and open-water races. You'll have to learn special skills: racing starts, Power 10s, and sprinting, as well as tactical considerations to help you do your best. When it comes to having a good experience,

however, the most critical issues are often the most mundane details. Rowing races are not nearly as simple logistically as running a marathon or bicycle racing. There are a lot more ways to screw up.

Probably the saddest rowers I've ever seen were the members of the 1979 U.S. lightweight four-without-coxswain at the 1979 World Championships in Bled, Yugoslavia. It was the morning of the first heat of the regatta, and the four looked very smooth from where I stood behind the starting platform as they approached the starting line. But they were late. Very late. It was a six-boat heat, with the six lanes marked by lines of buoys every 5 meters like lanes of a swimming pool. As in most championship events, the races were on a tight schedule. Each crew had to be on the starting line at least 2 minutes before the race was scheduled to begin.

When the two-minute warning was announced over the loudspeakers the U.S. crew appeared to be about 500 meters away down the course. When they finally arrived, a red flag hung over their lane marker to indicate that they had been assessed a false start for delaying the race. Two false starts meant disqualification. Unfortunately, the crew did not notice the penalty flag and did not understand the judge, who spoke in French. They must have been rattled, and wanted time to compose themselves. When the judge gave the sequence starting commands, "Etes-vous prêt? Partez!" the crew, who I had framed in the viewfinder of my camera, left the starting line on "êtes." Not surprisingly, they led the race off the line, but then judges' horns blew and the six boats all stopped. Only then did the U.S. crew realize that they already had the one false start and that their second meant disqualification. The judge ordered them to leave the starting area, and they watched the other crews line up to race without them. All that time and training—not to mention the cost of the trip to Yugoslavia—and they never got to compete.

Once you start to race, you will probably come to love it. Your only complaint will be the few occasions you get to do it. Don't let stupid mistakes ruin any of yours.

TO BE SURE YOU CAN START

USRA membership: To race in virtually every flat-water regatta in this country, as well as a growing number of open-water races, you must have a current membership in the United States Rowing Association—about $25 per year. Sometimes you can join the USRA at the regatta site, but don't count on it. Among other things, the USRA provides the insurance that makes regattas possible in our litigious times. You also get a sub-

scription to the excellent USRA magazine, *American Rowing*.

Club affiliation: For major events like the Head of the Charles, you must belong to a club affiliated with the USRA. In practice, club affiliations can be very tenuous. If your sister-in-law's roommate from summer camp rows for the Susquatch Rowing Club, you can probably get away with saying that you do too. If you win a medal, however, it will be mailed to the Susquatch Rowing Club and you may never see it. If you can't find a club in your area, you should contact the USRA about starting a new club.

In a sprint race your bow number is your lane number. At a head race, like the Head of the Charles, your number is your position in the starting lane. This shell is starting in first place, which means it probably won the event the previous year.

Register early: It is sometimes possible to get an entry for a small regatta on the day of the race, but even that is becoming more difficult. For the Head of the Charles, getting an entry at all can be like getting a number in the New York City Marathon. A lot more people want to compete than the event can hold. Race calendars and entry forms are often printed in *American Rowing*. Mail in your entries early.

If possible, pick up your registration materials the day before the regatta. Do it yourself. Running around a major regatta in search of the guy who picked up your number is no fun.

Bow numbers and body numbers: For most big races you must have a lane number or starting-position number mounted on the bow of your shell as well as on your back. Make sure you have a number clip mounted on your boat and then secure the number in the clip with duct tape. If your number falls off, you may be disqualified. Number clips and sets of lane numbers (1–6) are available from the USRA or from specialty shops.

Lightweight weigh-in: If the regatta has weight categories and you have entered in anything other than the open or heavyweight category, you must be weighed. The registration packet will tell you when and where.

Know your schedule: Get a map of the course and a schedule of the races as early as possible. Figure out in advance where you can store and launch your shell, where you can warm up, and what time you have to be at the starting line. The less you have to think about on race day, the better off you are. If at all possible, row over the course at least once before you race. Ask veterans what conditions to expect. On a winding course with narrow bridges such as the Head of the Charles, experience can make an enormous difference in your time.

Spare parts: Something invariably breaks before a race—anything from a shoelace to a footstretcher support. The more spare parts you have and the larger your roll of duct tape, the better off you will be.

Rig for the conditions: If the wind or water conditions are different from what you are used to, you'll have to adjust your rigging. If the water is rough, you'll have to raise the height of the oarlocks a centimeter or so. If there is a strong headwind blowing, you may want to lighten the load on your oars by moving your oar collars slightly. Be conservative with any changes. Check all your bolts and nuts. This is not a good time to experiment.

Before you launch: Regatta schedules are easily altered by bad weather, broken boats, computer malfunctions, and poor management. If your event is scheduled at ten-thirty in the morning, the only thing you can be reasonably sure of is that the race will not start *before* that time. Memorize the order of events before yours and keep track of them.

Break a light sweat before you get in your shell, either with an easy jog or some light calisthenics. If it is chilly, wear your sweat clothes, socks, and shoes until you are on the dock ready to launch. The shorter the race, the longer you may want to warm up in your boat. If it's a 2,000-meter race, you should allow at least half an hour of warmup on the water before you go to the line. Longer races may warrant less warmup—

Remember, if your number falls off you will be disqualified. Use your duct tape to make sure.

depending on your physical condition.

Your goal is to get to the line completely warmed up, and then have a couple of minutes to bail out your boat, make a final check of your equipment, shuck any extra clothing, and get your boat aligned. You don't want to sit on the starting line for a long time getting cold and nervous—especially if the boats you're racing against are not yet on the line. Veteran crews tend to be the last to arrive at the line. Part of that is strategic. Another part is that veterans take too many things for granted and often end up scrambling.

Water bottles and lemon wedges: On a hot day, a few sips of water before you race can be a great help with "cotton mouth." Better still, carry a couple of lemon or orange wedges to suck on just before the race. If you carry a water bottle on a short race, empty it before you start. Don't carry more weight than you have to.

SPRINT RACING

Sprint races are typically 2,000 meters, but occasionally Women's and Masters races are only 1,000 or 1,500 meters. The ideal course is like an enormous swimming pool protected from the wind and divided into six lanes marked by buoys spaced at 5-meter intervals. More common is a more-or-less straight course marked by a large buoy every 250 meters or so. The starting line is a stationary platform or moored "stake boat." A stake boat boy holds the stern of your shell. An aligner at the edge of the course makes sure that all the bows are in line.

When you're on the starting line of a major regatta, and the aligner has the bows of the boat in line, the starter will assume you are ready unless you have one hand raised in the air. Keep your hand up until your boat is aligned and you are ready for the starting commands.

Starting commands: "Are you ready? Ready All. Row!" Or sometimes, "Etes-vous prêt? Partez!" In general, inexperienced rowers will wait until they hear the word "row!" or "partez!" Veteran racers will often anticipate the last command and risk a false start.

When you're waiting on the starting line, have your oar blades flat on the water for stability. Before the starter says "row," however, your oar blades should be "squared and buried" in the water, ready to take the first stroke. Practice this in advance. Some scullers square their blades at the command, "Are you ready?" Decide on a strategy before you get to the line and then stick with it. Some people make a lot of noise when they square their blades, which can be distracting at the line. If you keep your mind on your own plan, you won't be rattled.

Countdown start: If there is a strong wind, especially a strong crosswind that pushes the boats out of alignment, the starter may call for a countdown start: "Five, four, three, two, one. Are you ready? Ready all. Row." Once the countdown starts, it will not stop even if you are blown off course. The key is to keep your bow pointed toward the wind at the beginning of the countdown, so that you drift into proper alignment by the word "Row!" Countdown starts are not very common. If the conditions require one, the race should probably be postponed. But it's worth practicing on windy days.

First three strokes: Your goal is to get the boat up to full speed as quickly as possible, which means taking several less-than-full-slide strokes. Your first three strokes should be at between one-half and three-quarter slides. "Half, half, three quarters" or "three quarters, half, three quarters" are both standard starts. The first three strokes are short and quick, but finish them completely to keep yourself balanced.

3, 20 - high, and settle—conventional starting wisdom: After the first three strokes to get your boat moving, the next ten or twenty strokes are typically rowed 4 or 5 strokes per minute higher than your normal cadence. Then, you "settle" to a pace sustainable for the "body" of the race. There are physiological and psychological reasons for rowing these first strokes so high. First of all, they may help to take an early lead and be able to see your competition. Also, there is some laboratory evidence that if you start an event at a very high intensity before you drop down to a more sustainable level, you will be able to expend more total energy during the event (and therefore finish the race faster) than if you start at a slower pace. Be very careful not to stay at a high cadence too long. Ten "high strokes" may be better for you than twenty. I have seen oarsmen row high for thirty strokes. The result is a "fly and die." They fly off the starting line and die soon after. One primary reason for the initial sprint is to allow you to settle down to the right pace. It's much easier to settle down after twenty strokes than it is to speed up.

The 30-second rule: At most 2,000-meter regattas, the judges will restart a race if your equipment breaks during the first 30 seconds or 250 meters. You should know the signal marking the end of the 30 seconds (a horn or a buoy at 250 meters). If your equipment breaks beyond that signal, you are out of luck. So if something breaks within the first 30 seconds, don't be bashful: start hollering. The closer the breakage is to the start, and the louder the hollering, the more likely the judge is to stop the race. In theory, a "jumped seat" or "catching a crab" is not considered equipment breakage and will not cause a restart. In reality, the 30-second rule has been known to cover mistakes.

The body of the race: Physiologically, an even pace throughout the race is the most efficient pace. Variations in the speed consume large amounts of extra energy. With that in mind, your strategy should be to row at the fastest pace that you can sustain for the length of the course. Your 500-meter split time should remain the same throughout the race. To row "even splits," however, you must expect to be behind in the first 1,500 meters or so, and then move ahead as the rest of the rowers fade.

Most racers don't have the confidence to row a steady pace. Their boat speed is much more erratic: fast in the first 500, slowing slightly in the second 500, and often slowing precipitously in the third 500. The final 500 is a sprint with whatever speed is left.

The better you know the course and all its landmarks and steering points, the better you will race. It can help to bring a map with you for your practices.

Special Moves: Power 10s and Flutter 10s

Theoretically, every stroke in a race is at full pressure, but some strokes can be "fuller" than others. On a Power 10 your goal is to increase your speed as much as possible for ten strokes. A couple of Power 10s at planned points in the race can be very useful for maintaining your concentration. Power 10s can also be useful when you are passing another boat. The more Power 10s you use in a race, the less useful they are. You have to be very careful not to slack off before or after the power move.

A Flutter 10 is a more radical and dangerous move. On a flutter you raise your stroke rating a couple of beats for ten strokes or so. Fluttering can help you break away from the pack, but it will burn an enormous amount of extra energy (and douse you with lactic acid). If you don't reap an equally enormous benefit from your effort, the result will be disastrous.

Sprinting: The conventional strategy is something like this: You row the first 1,500 meters and then look around. If you are not winning, you raise your stroke rating one stroke per minute and hold that rate for another 250 meters. Still not in front? Raise your stroke rating higher and higher until you are. This strategy works in a couple of ways: If you win, that's wonderful. If you don't, the extra effort leaves you so wiped out that you don't care.

For inexperienced rowers, sprinting loses races as often as it wins them. It is very easy to fool yourself by raising the rate. The stroke rate may come up, but the boat does not move any faster—and sometimes it even slows down. If you plan to sprint in a race, you have to practice sprinting—and practice when you are tired!

Sprint technique: The goal is to apply power as fast as possible with the strongest muscles (the legs) and minimize time spent pulling with the weakest muscles (the arms). That can be done by cutting down on body swing (reducing the angle at the catch and finish) and removing the blade from the water with a reduced arm draw (reducing the angle at the finish). In other words, sit up straight and concentrate on getting your legs into the drive as fast as possible.

HEAD RACING

Head racing is generally a lot less formal and a lot more fun than sprint racing. The boats race single file over a distance of 2 to 4 miles. From the bank a head race looks more like a parade, but on the course it feels like many separate races are going on at the same time. Ultimately, the race is against the clock, but you don't know your time as you row, and the official results are not tabulated for several hours or even days after the event. The greatest thrill and glory of rowing in the Head of the Charles is to overtake crews in front of you—to shuffle the sequence of bow numbers so that your boat, number 12, passes the reviewing stand in the wake of number 8.

A few minutes before the start of a head race the boats cluster above the starting line and begin to line up, single file, according to the bow numbers. There is typically a "chute" marked by buoys before the actual starting line. You don't need a "racing start." The number 1 boat (usually last year's winner) starts rowing at the beginning of the chute and builds to full pressure by the time it reaches the starting line. The number 2 boat (last year's second place) follows about 10 seconds behind, followed by number 3, and so on. The slower boats and new entries are at the tail of the line. The only strategy at the beginning of the chute is to stay as close as possible to the boat in front of you and perhaps take a Power 10 as you cross the starting line. It can be a tremendous boost to pass another crew early in the race. On the other hand, head races are long, and a steady pace is critical. Remember, these are 80%-intensity races, not 100%.

Skill, cunning, and a time handicap can make the old-timers hard to beat.

Whoever dies with the most T-shirts, wins.

Other than being in good shape, the most critical factor in head racing is experience on the course. For example, the Head of the Charles is well marked with buoys, and you'll see the veterans rowing right along them, cutting the turns as tightly as possible. It's a risky maneuver: Your oar blades can cross over a buoy, but if your hull crosses the buoy, you will be penalized by 15 seconds. If you don't know the course well,

you have to stay farther away from the buoys and that will cost you time.

Head racing is completely unpredictable—especially if you are new to the event and start at the tail. You may overtake several boats or be overtaken. You may suffer a collision, or have to row off course to get around another collision. Keep your sense of humor and pull as best you can. The best revenge is to have as much fun as possible while you row.

OPEN-WATER RACES

In California, around Marina del Rey, Santa Cruz, and Sausalito, in particular, the sport of recreational rowing is being stretched and transformed. Scullers have taken to the waves, surfing their shells. Races have become endurance adventures out of sight of land. The Ironman of open-water rowing is California Yacht Club's Catalina to Marina del Rey Rowing and Paddling Derby, a 32-nautical mile adventure that started in 1977, but most open-water regattas offer a choice of long, rough courses for experts and shorter, more sheltered courses for novices. Open-water rowing is still a small segment of the sport. The Catalina Race attracts less than one hundred entries, but its effect on the sport and boat development is profound.

The first things you'll notice about serious open-water racing boats is the life jacket fastened to the bow and the compass mounted on the stern. You learn quickly about how waves break over shells. You learn about bailing techniques and the limits of self-bailers and why a life jacket is required. In long races, you have to worry about navigation when fog or sheer distance has obscured your point. You learn firsthand about carrying water and the perils of dehydration (see Staying Fluid, page 98). The closest I've been to a long open-water race was the 34-mile Round Manhattan Race in four-oared shells. I learned that it is possible to shiver with fatigue and cold while rowing at full pressure. On the other hand, there is no better feeling than to finish a very long race. In the next edition of this book I plan to report firsthand on open-water rowing. In the meantime, if you have particular suggestions on open-water rowing, or any type of rowing, please let me know by writing The Rowing Machine Companion.

ON CHOOSING A RACING PARTNER

A pliable character who submits readily to the will of his coach is quick to learn and pleasant to deal with, but his pliability may, and often does, imply a fatal readiness to yield to an adversary's will on the day of battle.—GILBERT BOURNE, *A Textbook on Oarsmanship*

Any damn fool can start on the word "go," but it takes experience to start on the word "Are . . ."—anonymous Oxford blue

---

TED NASH'S GREAT SHARK ATTACK OF 1984

Ted Nash, head coach of the Pennsylvania Athletic Club (Penn A. C.), is one of the most successful rowing coaches in the country—and perhaps the most colorful, controversial, and sometimes even the most inspirational coach I've met. In the last few years his boats have brought home several World Medals. In 1984 I had the opportunity to row for Ted at Penn A. C. I saved his instruction sheet from the Olympic trials.

> Bring race shirt / white hat
> Extra rain rowing gear
> Sneaks if first set is wet
> Casuals for cookout
> Sweat top (on a cool day)

- Take care of your own boat parts, riggers/oars.
- Mark all parts with name of boat and seat number.
- T.A.N. will provide bow markers.
- T.A.N. will have cold drinks and cups, ice, etc. H_2O, some bottles for water in boats. Drink *a lot* of H_2O.
- T.A.N. will have bow splash plates/tape/tools, sponges.
- All shells when rigged will be tied on frame rack or trailer—REMOVE SEATS.
- Be on time, professional, save energy by quiet, efficient work.
- Return tools to wood toolbox as soon as you have done your work so others can use them.
- We are there to win, not bitch about course, officials, or system. We will win under *any* system. Shark symbol is in full use. Feeding frenzy is in full force.
- Take *no* medicine unless you see T.A.N. If you are now on medication, have doctor's letter of use and an okay. All winners will be tested and if not under medical letters, an offender may be kicked off U.S. Team then.
- See T.A.N. for any (even slight) injury. T.A.N. will have first-aid supplements in van.

—'84 in L.A. *is* sweet.

The Coach

Appendix I
A ROWER'S TIMELINE

427 B.C. The Greek historian Thucydides tells us that one Greek trireme (a three-tiered rowing ship crammed with about 170 oarsmen and 30 soldiers) pursued another to the city of Mytilene on Lesbos in order to deliver a command reversing a previous order to destroy the city. The ship set a record unequaled since.

Circa 944 A.D. Britain's King Edgar the Peaceful serves as coxswain when provincial kings row him down the River Dee, the last recorded incident of any coxswain being dubbed the Peaceful.

1661 Samuel Pepys, English diarist, records that a boat race is sculled on the Thames during which "upon the start, the wager boats fall foul of one another till at last one of them gives over, pretending foul play, and so the other rowed away alone and all our sport lost."

1721 English actor Thomas Doggett dies, leaving a will that declares a race should be held annually "forever," with prizes being his ornate coat and a badge. The custom is begun, with Doggett's Coat and Badge Race remaining Britain's longest sporting competitive tradition.

1752 Renowned mathematician Leonhard Euler publishes the first treatise on how the oar works. To this day no one seems completely sure.

1775 First regatta is held on the Thames, a pageant-like spectacle borrowing from the splendors of Venetian banners and feasts, teaches Londoners that rowing need not only be a brutish competition among professional watermen. A contemporary chronicler records, "Bad liquor, in short measure, was plentifully retailed."

1782 A race on the Thames, during which two oarsmen kept "pretty near abreast of each other till they came pretty nigh the goal . . . [then the] first man's scull split, which retarded him so much that the second man got in first."

1788   Two rowing eights face each other on the Thames, starting at Westminster and finishing at Richmond. The "exertions were so great after this encounter that one man may be said to have died on his oar and two others, on being landed at Kew, were taken very ill."

1795   At a Thames race, where crowds typically riot, a spectator is killed by a flying bottle.

1811   Some students at Eton College take to the river in a ten-oared boat, labeled the *Monarch*.

1817   Students at Eton get around to staging a boat race.

1818   The bunch who held the first race at Eton went to Oxbridge, where they started rowing there, too.

1829   The first Oxford-Cambridge Race is held, founded by, among others, the nephew of the poet William Wordsworth. There is no record of whether the man who wrote "I wandered lonely as a cloud" ever wandered over to witness a boat race. The first Oxford-Cambridge boat weighed 600 pounds.

1839   Royal Henley Regatta first rowed on the Thames; now the Wimbledon or Ascot of rowing.

1846   Iron outriggers are first introduced in races, for the Oxford-Cambridge Race. As a result, much longer and narrower boats become the style, up to 66' long and with a beam of only 2' or less wide.

1852   First Harvard-Yale Boat Race begins intercollegiate sport competition in America.

1857   At the Oxford-Cambridge Boat Race, an eight without a keel is first used. A smooth skin further cut down on the weight of the boat.

1870   A moving seat is first used at the Hudson River Regatta. With the moving seat, rowers increase the length of the stroke and legs play a much more important part in the process.

1871   The young American painter Thomas Eakins begins his series of great rowing pictures with his portrait *Max Schmitt in a Single Scull*. Eakins' dozens of rowing pictures and sketches have never been rivaled as painterly expressions of the sport.

1872   The National Association of Amateur Oarsmen is formed to combat the pernicious effect of professional rowing in America. The pros are vicious competitors, not above sawing an opponent's shell in half before a major race!

1876   The American rowing author Ed Brickwood writes in *Boat Racing*, "Good oarsmanship is not confined to the male sex." Women are rowing at Wellesley College in 1877. And in 1888, an oarswoman, Mollie King of Newport, Kentucky, issued a public challenge to other women rowers for a "two-mile race for stakes."

1877   Edward Hanlan faces Charles Courtney in one of the great pro rowing matches in American history. Hanlan wins and the rematch is canceled when Courtney's boat is hacked in half.

1882   Philadelphia's Boathouse Row is crowned with its architectural gem, the Undine Barge Club's boathouse, designed by the masterful American architect Frank Furness.

1890 First nonstationary rowing machines. Called a Road Sculler, the machine is a go-cart, propelled by a rower using pulleys connected to large wheels. These devices are used by pros for Madison Square Garden road races, go-as-you-please races, which admit any wheeled vehicle.

1900 First rowing in the Olympics. This was the second modern-day Olympics, but the first had weather so bad that rowing was canceled. The American eight won the Gold Medal, the Vesper Club of Philadelphia taking the honors. From 1920 to 1956 U.S. crews won the Gold for the eights in every Olympics.

1907 A semi-failure of a baseball coach, Hiram Conibear, finds a job as crew coach at the University of Washington. To everyone's surprise, perhaps even his own, he uses skeletons to develop theories that revolutionize rowing and brings to glory the great boatbuilder George Pocock.

1908 At the Olympics a British crew of "old crocks" triumphs, led by 42-year-old Guy Nickalls, who had won at Henley before his crew's stroke was even born.

1919 Jack Kelly, Sr., of the Vesper Club, is refused admission to Henley's *Diamond Sculls* because the Henley stewards have waged a longtime feud against Vesper for its semi-pro competitions. Kelly, however, takes his exclusion as a class judgment against his origins as an Irish manual laborer. Kelly, father of the late Princess Grace of Monaco and her brother, Jack Kelly, Jr., also a great oarsman, would do much to propagate the Henley class myth in the years to come.

1920 British coach Steve Fairbairn begins his worldwide popularity as row-ing sage and personality. He advocates the "natural" approach instead of the "orthodox" style then popular. Because it is easier and often more productive to row à la Fairbairn, his ideas catch on.

1960 Karl Adam, innovative German coach, begins receiving a string of Olympic Gold medals with his Ratzeburg crew. Adam's methods, learned partly from his experiences with boxing, include interval training, or what the Germans call *fährtespiel*.

1964 Boston's Head of the Charles Race begins. Modeled on London's Head of the Thames Race (founded in the 1920s by Cambridge coach Steve Fairbairn), the Head of the Charles soon becomes a uniquely American event. The race finds room for everyone from the most able college crews to "old farts out to have some fun."

1972 The University of Oregon Webfoot crew is coxed by a woman, Vicky Brown, a landmark step in the career of women coxswains. The sports pages report that, according to the NCAA, "girls are not allowed to compete in men's sports." In a few short years, women everywhere would almost be granted the right to compete in boys' sports.

1972 Arthur Martin markets the first Alden Ocean Shell, a revolutionary step in the popularity of the stable, seaworthy single scull.

1976 The Yale women's crew, fed up with getting second-class treatment from the athletics department, strip to the buff in the athletic director's office with the words TITLE IX outlined in Yale-blue magic marker on their fronts and backs. (Title IX guaranteed equal funding for men's and women's sports. The ensuing publicity helped to raise funds for an addition to the boathouse.)

1978   Carbon fiber oars are developed by the Dreissigacker Brothers of Vermont and used by Yale in the Eastern Sprints, to win their first championship since 1963. The lighter, more durable oars mean less maintenance time and less weight carried in the boat.

1982   The CRASH-B sprints on Concept II ergometers are first held in Cambridge, Massachusetts. The merry get-together begins with all the maritime dignity of *Gilligan's Island.* CRASH-B has grown into the World Indoor Rowing Championships. In 1988, the Soviet Union sends a team.

1988   A 1985 replica of an ancient trireme attempts unsuccessfully to match the trireme speed record set in 427 B.C.

*T*he story of English rowing in the twentieth century resembles that of the great religious wars of history . . . rival dogmas, supported with all the force of unreasoning fanaticism, even rival religious symbolism . . . probably at no time in the history of English rowing have more people rowed worse than today.—PETER HAIG-THOMAS and M. A. NICHOLSON, *The English Style of Rowing: New Light on an Old Method*

Appendix II
ROWING SCHOOLS

Adventure Fitness
12 Queen Street
Lakefield, Ontario
K0L 2H0 Canada
(705) 652-7986

Blue Heron Rowing Club
0425 Southwest Montgomery Street
Suite 110
Portland, OR 97201
(503) 223-5859

Craftsbury Sculling Center
P.O. Box 31
Craftsbury Common, VT 05827
(802) 586-2514

Durham Boat Company
R.F.D. 2
Newmarket Road
Durham, NH 03824
(603) 659-2548

Florida Rowing School
Sandpiper Bay Resort
Port St. Lucie, FL 33452
(305) 335-4400

Open Water Rowing Company
Foot of Spring Street
Sausalito, CA 94965
(415) 332-1091

Rowing/NW
3304 Fuhrman Avenue E
Seattle, WA 98102
(206) 324-5800

Small Boat Gallery
48 Garrett Road
Upper Darby, PA 19082
(215) 352-9595

Santa Cruz Rowing School
P.O. Box 7782
Santa Cruz, CA 95062
(open-water rowing)

Sparhawk Sculling School
222 Porters Point Road
Colchester, VT 05446
(802) 658-4799

Trent Sculling School
Trent University
Peterborough, Ontario
K9J 7B8 Canada
(705) 748-1260

Appendix III
BOAT-BUILDERS, SUPPLIERS, AND REPAIRERS

(See also Boat Buyer's Guide, pages 19–25).

Source	Product
Boathouse Row Sports 1021 Ridge Avenue Philadelphia, PA 19123 (215) 769-0769	Complete line of clothing gear.
Canadian Amateur Rowing Assoc. (CARA) 333 River Road Tower C, 10th floor Vanier, Ontario K1L 8B9 Canada (613) 746-5758	Development material includes coaching and *Catch* magazine.
Composite Engineering Van Dusen Racing Boats 742 Main Street Winchester, MA 01890 (617) 721-2156	Competitive and recreational singles, doubles, and pairs. Boat covers, racks, complete line of sculling accessories, drop-in rowing units, coaching launches.
Concept II Dreissigacker Racing Oars R.R. 1 Box 1100 Morrisville, VT 05661 (800) 245-5676	Oars, oarlocks and ergs.
Hudson Racing Shells 90 Cliftonvale Avenue London, Ontario N6J 1J8 Canada	Racing shells—singles, doubles, pairs, straight four, cox four, and quad (wood and plastic).

Hurka National Laboratories
41 W. 042 Colson Drive
St. Charles, IL 60174

Recreational and racing singles. Kevlar sculling oars. Lubrication and low-friction hull coating.

Ibex Boat Company
541 Pelham Road
New Rochelle, NY
(914) 636-9717
(914) 235-6556

Carbon fiber racing shells—singles, doubles, and pairs.

Kaschper Racing Shells
P.O. Box 40
Lucan, Ontario
NOM 230 Canada
(519) 227-4652

Full line of racing shells, parts, and trailers.

King Boat Works
P.O. Box 273
South Woodstock, VT 05071
(802) 457-1075

Lightweight training singles; shell repairs; shell trailers.

Nielsen-Kellerman Company
1066 High Vista Trail
Webster, NY 14580
(716) 671-8592

Strokecoach: One-stroke rate computer, stroke counter, and automatic timer. Carrying case included. Waterproof and floatable.

Chronostroke: Digital stroke watch with memory stopwatch. Saves 8 cumulative *and* 8-lap split times. Waterproof and flotable.

Onboard Products
459 Main Street
Amesbury, MA 01913
(617) 388-0162

Onboard Sliding Feet Rower, a self-contained rower, turns a canoe, sailboard, or other small boat into a rowing craft. Attaches without tools or modification.

Owen Racing Shells
P.O. Box 1167
Sisters, OR 97759
(503) 549-7702

Racing singles, doubles, and pairs. Wherries, sculling oars, and boat covers for the above.

Piantedosi Oars
P.O. Box 643
West Acton, MA 01720
(617) 263-1814

Wooden and composite sweep and sculling oars, canoe and skiff conversions; rowing ergometers.

Rower's Bookshelf
P.O. Box 440
Essex, MA 01929
(508) 468-4096

See the Complete Recreational Rower's Library (page 144).

Rowing Crafters
520 Waldo Point
Sausalito, CA 94965
(415) 332-3577

Recreational and traditional singles and doubles. Trainers (builder/dealer). Publisher of "California Open-Water Rowing Association Newsletter."

The Rowing Machine Companion
c/o 502 Woodhaven Court
Aptos, CA 95003

Home video for ergometers or rowing machines that simulates rowing in a U.S. Team quadruple scull on the Charles River in Boston. Four complete workouts. $42.95 includes shipping.

Sport Book Publishers
278 Robert Street
Toronto, Ontario
Canada M55 ZK8
(416) 922-0860

Publishers of *Rowing/Rudern, The Complete Sculler,* and *A Textbook of Oarsmanship.*

USRA Clearing House
201 S. Capitol Avenue
Indianapolis, IN 46225
(317) 237-5656

American Rowing Magazine, racing memberships, as well as the USRA clearing house, a full line of rowing clothing, sweaters, hats, T-shirts, decals, books, bumper stickers, pins, etc. Write for free catalogue.

Vespoli USA
98 Columbus Street
Hamden, CT
(203) 773-0311

Full line of racing and recreational shells in both Carbon/Honeycomb and Carbon Fiberglas laminate construction. Parts and fittings available. Write for new boat and/or parts brochure.

Appendix IV
THE COMPLETE RECREATIONAL ROWER'S LIBRARY

Most of these books are no longer available in bookstores, but many of them can be purchased by mail from Pat Smith at The Rowers Bookshelf, Box 440-W, Essex, MA 01929. Or call (508) 468-4096 and Pat will send you a catalogue. Otherwise contact Peter Klavora at Sports Book.

Gilbert Bourne. *A Textbook on Oarsmanship*, Oxford University Press, 1923. Reprinted in 1987 by Sports Book Publishers, Toronto. Intelligent guide by an anatomist, still read and appreciated by rowing fans many years after its first publication. Bourne was gifted with literary skill and a sense of humor, rare attributes in experts on rowing technique.

Gilbert Bourne. *Memories of an Eton Wet-Bob of the Seventies:* Oxford University Press, 1933. Posthumously published, these reminiscences must count among the most charming ever written on rowing. A wet-bob in British parlance is sim-ply a rower; a dry-bob would be a rugby footballer.

Bruce C. Brown. *Stroke! A Guide to Recreational Rowing:* Camden, ME, International Marine Publishing, 1986. A serious and responsible brief book on how to get started in open-water rowing.

Bruce C. Brown. *Long Strokes:* Camden, ME, International Marine Publishing, 1986. A very useful guide to open-water cruising and distance racing.

Richard Burnell. *The Complete Sculler:* Marlow, England Simpson, 1977. Reprinted by Sports Books, Toronto. A capable appraisal of the sculling situation by one of the writing deans of the sport.

David Churbuck. *The Book of Rowing:* Woodstock, NY, Overlook Press, 1988. A personal look at the sport with some attractive black-and-white historical photos.

Hylton Cleaver. *A History of Rowing:*

London, Herbert Jenkins, 1957. An amusingly snobby volume about rowing in Britain, and mostly at Henley. The book dates to the height of the Cold War, so there are plenty of outraged comments about Russians and their "invasion" of Henley and other bastions of English rowing.

Christopher Dodd. *The Oxford and Cambridge Boat Race:* London, Stanley Paul, 1983. Prolific British journalist offers the most up-to-date, chatty book on the subject. Many diverting quotes from older, hard-to-find volumes. Dodd is obviously someone who loves the sport very much, and this appreciation helps enliven his books.

Christopher Dodd. *The Henley Royal Regatta:* London, Stanley Paul, 1981. Along the same lines as his valuable Oxford-Cambridge book, Dodd scores again with more nostalgic quotes, and many inside jokes about the great Brit institution of Henley.

H. R. A. Edwards. *The Way of a Man with a Blade:* London, Routledge & Kegan Paul, 1963. A rather pompous and self-serious study by a noted British coach, nicknamed "Jumbo" by his oarsmen.

Steve Fairbairn. *On Rowing:* London, Nicholas Kaye, 1951. Another famous English coach, this one from Cambridge. Fairbairn emphasized achievement over form per se, incurring the wrath of those who disagreed with him, but winning the allegiance of amateur hammer rowers everywhere who didn't care all that much about form to begin with. Fairbairn was famous worldwide at one time.

John A. Ferriss, ed. *Rowing Fundamentals: A Manual for Coaches:* Indianapolis, United States Rowing Association. Fairly technical, authoritative articles by noted American coaches on how to excel in competitive rowing.

David Halberstam. *The Amateurs:* New York, William Morrow, 1985. Pulitzer Prize–winner Halberstam looks on some American rowers' quest for the 1984 Olympics. Contains valuable sketches of fine rowers such as John Biglow, Joe Bouscaren, Brad Lewis, and Paul Enquist.

Ernst Herberger. *Rowing (Rudern)*—The German Democratic Republic text of oarsmanship, ed. and trans. by Peter Klavora: Toronto, Sports Books, 1987, 4th ed. A formidable illustration of the kind of organized training that makes the East Germans a fearsome force in contemporary rowing. For contorted prose style, this one would be hard to beat.

Robert Herrick. *Red Top:* Cambridge, MA, Harvard University Press, 1948. The author is not the seventeenth-century British poet, but a true believer in the Harvard crew who has assembled much team history here. Most importantly, a good bibliography of rowing literature is included for the serious researcher on rowing.

Ronnie Howard. *Knowing Rowing:* San Diego, A. S. Barnes, 1977. British coach, disciple of "Jumbo" Edwards, contributes a useful book that is short on text but long on photos of a rower, Nigel Hunt, showing just about every posture a rower might find himself in.

Benjamin Ivry. *Regatta: An Illustrated Look at Rowing*, foreword by Stephen Kiesling: New York, Simon & Schuster, 1988. An unconventional look at the sport by a non-rower; plenty of poetic quotes and unlikely notes; certainly one of the funniest volumes on a serious activity.

Robert Kelly. *American Rowing:* New York, Putnam's, 1932. Despite its age, this book still retains considerable relaxed charm. The author, a journalist, dug up some amusing facts and photos from around the turn of the century.

Stephen Kiesling. *The Shell Game:* New York, William Morrow, 1982. A must.

Barbara Kirch. *Row for Your Life:* New York, Simon & Schuster, 1985. Unintimidating introduction to the sport, especially focused on rowing for handicapped persons, older athletes, and other non-Olympians. Information a bit dated.

Peter Klavora. *Rowing 1:* Toronto, Canadian Amateur Rowing Association, 1984. National Coaching Certification Program. Outstanding guide for coaches, written in a highly popular style, complete with cartoons and other morale-boosting amusements.

Charles Kuntzleman. *Rowing Machine Workouts:* Chicago, Contemporary Books, 1985.

R. C. Lehmann. *Anni Fugaces:* London, The Bodley Head, 1901. Ludicrously bad verse about rowing; there's a lot of really wretched doggerel about the sport that makes diverting reading today.

R. C. Lehmann. *The Complete Oarsman:* London, Methuen, 1908. When Lehmann said complete he meant complete; mainly notable for its amazing length, this book finds room for practically every turn-of-the-century rowing authority to gas on at length about the activity they loved. Most compelling are the reflections of such coaches as Guy Nickalls.

Devin Mahony. *The Challenge:* Chicago, Contemporary Books, 1989. A fine first-person account of the first woman coxswain of the Harvard Men's Varsity Crew.

Tom Mendenhall. *A Short History of American Rowing:* Cambridge, MA, Charles River Press, 1981. Those seeking reliable lists of victories in important crew races over many years would find it hard to find a source with more acumen than this book. The author is also a notable collector of memorabilia, a bit of which is illustrated therein.

Gordon Newell. *Ready All! George Yeoman Pocock and Crew Racing:* Seattle, University of Washington Press, 1987. Attractively large-format book about one of the great boatbuilders of all time. Pocock worked hand in hand with the legendary coach Hiram Conibear to establish Washington's famous rowing faculty. At one point, Pocock's wooden boats, made of the finest materials, were used by every rower. Nowadays, in the era of Fiberglas, some rowers still prefer the wood-boat experience and Pocock Boatbuilders carry on the family tradition of quality merchandising.

Guy Nickalls. *Life's a Pudding:* London, Faber and Faber, 1939. Don't be put off by the trifling title. Nickalls was one of the grand old men of English rowing, and his book is appealingly literate. It could hardly have been otherwise, published by Faber in the days when T. S. Eliot was one of the company directors.

Gully Nickalls. *A Rainbow in the Sky:* London, Chatto and Windus, 1974. Guy's son inherited his father's rowing talent and coaching skills, as well as the penchant for florid book titles. However, the poetic quote is apt, as the author, Wordsworth's nephew, was one of the founders of the Oxford-Cambridge Boat Race, which plays an important part in Nickalls' memoirs.

Irene Ward Norsen. *The Ward Brothers, Champions of the World:* New York, Vantage Press, 1958. A hugely admiring view of these nineteenth-century American idols, worshiped by the painter Thomas Eakins and other fans of the sport. The author is related to the Wards and is rightly proud of the family connection. Some amusing group portraits show the brothers looking a mite scrawny by modern standards, but decidedly tough and determined customers.

Michael Purcer. *Rigging*, Erie, PA, Qwik Press, 1987, 2nd ed. Useful, no-frills study, just how-to, directly and simply. Very pricey for what you get.

Daniel Topolski. *Boat Race: The Oxford Revival:* London, Collins Willow, 1985. Longtime Oxford coach, freelance journalist, and photographer, Topolski contributes an amusingly ribald study of the boat race.

Daniel Topolski. *True Blue:* London, Doubleday, 1989. To be inordinately kind, this is a too-close-to-be-objective version of the 1987 Oxford mutiny.

Edmund Warre. *On the Grammar of Rowing:* Oxford, Clarendon Press, 1909. Unbelievably stuffy excursus on the theory of rowing, full of Latin quotes, which even in 1909 must have been incomprehensible to most rowers. The continuing popularity of this volume is difficult to explain, unless it is due to the persistent intellectualization of rowing by certain academics.

Periodicals

American Rowing. The magazine of the USRA. 201 S. Capitol Avenue, Suite 400, Indianapolis, IN 46225. Subscription to the magazine is included with membership in the USRA.

"California Open-Water Rowing Association Newsletter." Yacht Fair Haven, Foot of Spring Street, Sausalito, CA 94965.

"Messing About in Boats." Published twice monthly on small-boat cruising; 29 Burley Street, Wenham, MA

Small Boat Journal. All kinds of small boats. P.O. Box 400, Route 9 West, Bennington, VT 05201.

Acknowledgments

Benjamin Ivry, Nike, The Craftsbury Sculling School, Steve Wagner, Marlene Royle, Concept II, John Ferris, The United States Rowing Association, Greg Sabourin, *Row* magazine, Mike Vespoli, Judy Geer, Matthew Labine, John Biglow, Joe Bouscaren, Tony Johnson, Kevin Sauer, Miguel Perez, Paula Oyer, and Brandt Aymar. With special thanks to E. C. "Ned" Frederick, Ph.D., president, Exeter Research, Inc.

Index